SYNCOPATED
RHYTHM

SYNCOPATED RHYTHM

*Recalibrating to Request by Faith, Recognize with Wisdom, and
Receive in Abundance the Desires of Your Heart*

PAMELA NORTH

XULON PRESS

Xulon Press
2301 Lucien Way #415
Maitland, FL 32751
407.339.4217
www.xulonpress.com

Unless otherwise indicated, scripture quotations taken from the
Holy Bible, New International Version (NIV). Copyright © 1973,
1978, 1984, 2011 by Biblica, Inc.™. Used by permission. All rights
reserved.

Printed in the United States of America.

ISBN-13: 978-1-6305-0401-4

For my wildest heartbeats
John, Alexander, Zechariah and Josiah

May you always march triumphantly to the beat of
God's heart.

CONTENTS

INTRODUCTION

E very story has substance. Your story matters, and so does mine. My story is not void of hardship and trials, but beautifully built upon them. The most challenging places I've traveled have grounded me to lean into Jesus and learn life's most valuable lessons.

We read and listen to the accounts of others and we laugh until our cheeks hurt. We cry until our faces are unrecognizable. We can become green with envy toward some and we are stirred to gratefulness that our feet never walked the paths of many. The lessons we learn from the chronicles of others can motivate us, thrust us into thanksgiving, or perhaps leave us wondering what our lives would be like if only things had been different. The beauty of our individual histories is the uniqueness that makes them our own; yet the commonalities that connect us with others echo in our hearts and engage us into community and family that strengthen, encourage and edify each other.

When I became a mother through adoption, I wanted to shout from the mountaintop and show off to the world what God had orchestrated. My desire was to start an epidemic of hope for mothers, fathers and children all in need of each other.

Cloud nine was my residence for months after our boys came home, and as often as possible, we would attend seminars and share our story to stir others' hearts for children all over the world in need of a family. The elation of being a mom has never vanished, but cloud nine evaporated quickly as the everyday challenges and responsibilities of raising children became a reality.

Overnight, our family of two doubled with two toddling baby boys, ages two and three. Our lives were turned upside down in a blissful way, and after two years the adoption bug bit again and we became a family of five. Life was crazy good-and some days it was just unadorned crazy.

Life is still a daily wonder of wild. Our boys are now teenagers, and as of a few days ago I can officially say we have three high schoolers. We have faced, and continue to face, some difficult, uphill, and frontline battles, but we keep climbing with a backpack of lessons learned along the way.

My desire to shout our story to the world was hushed until a few years ago. God reignited the spark in my heart to begin writing and I am so thankful that my fears didn't blow it out.

These words tumble off the pedestal of perfection, flailing frantically to make their way from my heart to these pages, but I have clung tenaciously to the Author of my story and the Perfecter of my faith to make a way for these words to reach you.

Lean in close for a peek of my journey thus far. I hope you laugh and cry, celebrate and dance, but most of all I hope you feel the thundering heartbeat of God.

May each of us be roused daily to delight in God and love him more. He will reveal desires in your heart you have yet to recognize and He will bless those desires to blossom into beauty you could never imagine on your own.

Loads of love, huge hugs, and bountiful blessings to you, my new friend.

"Reading through David's Psalms always leaves me with a hunger and desire for God. It is not so much a man's journey that defines him, but his destination, and David's destination was God." A. W. Tozer.[1]

Chapter 1

SAY CHEESE: A SNAPSHOT OF MY STORY

" ...and he will give you the desires of your heart."
Psalm 37:4 ESV

*T*he *Dreamers* is a print by Albert Joseph Moore that hangs over my mama's sofa. The artist captures four women sitting on a sofa, two of them have their heads nodded over with their left ears nearly resting on their shoulders. They appear to be sleeping. The older woman's head is resting on the back of the sofa, her eyes a speck open, I suspect due to her curiosity. At first glance, you might miss the other young woman, to the far right of the photo, her legs curled up, bare feet exposed, and her face hidden behind a pleated fan.

My mama gets tickled when she looks at this picture because she sees herself and her sisters, Ruby (no doubt the curious one) and Eloise. It was months before she noticed the young woman in the corner of the picture, and when she saw it, she exclaimed, "There's my Pamela, hiding in the corner!"

This print captures the quintessence of a hereditary gene in our family. We are not lazy women who sleep all the time, but we sprint about our daily duties so hard and so fast that when we finally sit, we succumb to slumber. Horizontal is not a requirement.

I've pondered while looking at this picture through the years and considered the dreams of the women exemplified in it. The reflection on their faces reveals the likelihood of sweet and peaceful dreams; but I have inside knowledge of the reality of the lives of these women and I wonder, do peace and contentment arrive only in our dreams?

The drifting desires in my heart as a young girl were simple. The playground where my dreams breathed life into my future included a stage on which my wish upon a star to become a country music superstar spotlighted my future vision of fame and fortune. Visions of myself in a purple-sequined jumpsuit, white boots with tassels, and a rhinestone-studded cowgirl hat belting out *These Boots are Made for Walking, Coal Miner's Daughter,* or *Delta Dawn* to a cheering audience of what I thought was one, the girl in the mirror, met an early curtain call. Weapons of laughter reached my ears, created a flood-gate of tears, and bruised my heart. The show was over, but the seeds for emotional strongholds of rejection and insecurity were just beginning to bind up this wounded, young warrior.

But there was another dream that jeers from peers would never wrestle from my heart. The bounty of baby dolls and stuffed animals snuggled in my bedroom personified the desire of my heart, which was to be the mother of bundles of babies. My dolls and animals lined up in my bedroom waiting to be fed, changed, and rocked to sleep as I sang sweet lulla-bies or read them a bedtime story.

Simple dreams for a young girl, but it was one heart's desire that tagged along and grew stronger and more secure with each beat of my heart.

Playtime was not expended on tending to my "children" or belting out tunes using the finial from my canopy bed as a microphone. I had an adventurous wild zone where my cousin Connie was constant in guiding me to explore nature and take mischievous tomboy risks that included bike races, jumping ditches, rowing boats in the Pamlico River and getting stuck in muck up to our eyeballs in the canal, scraping elbows, and skinning knees all to ensure equalization to my prissy side.

No matter the winding paths of adventure in a day, the little mama branded on my heart made sure all my babies and stuffed animals were snuggled in for the night. My mama had legitimate concerns that I would suffocate during the night surrounded by so much batting, cotton, plastic pellets, and beans. Most little ones have a security blanket. I had a security force.

Indubitably, I was not alone in my fairy tale dreams. Little girls dream of being mamas and start planning their weddings before they reach their tweens. Images of Prince Charming, a house surrounded by a white picket fence, and the pitter-patter of little feet running around the house are nestled in their noggins. My personal Prince Charming was a hybrid of Ken (the perfect match for Barbie) and a rugged cowboy who would rustle up his little lady and ride off with her into the sunset to live happily ever after.

HAPPILY EVER AFTER

They were good things, this life plan of mine. Life, neatly packaged and secured with a huge pink satin bow. Even though these dreams and desires seemed clear in my simple mind, my vision was blurred past the white picket fence that surrounded and protected the domain in my dreams. God's dream for our lives is so much more than the ordinary performance of the perfect "American dream." God knew I needed so much more than this perfect ordinary life to prepare me for the perfect storms brewing in my extraordinary future and in the futures of those I met on the crossroads. I needed growth, maturity, wisdom, compassion, confidence, and so much more. I needed to be raised up by my Perfect Father in a way that would teach me to offer hope and love to others in our broken world.

Mark Batterson, NY Times bestselling author, wrote the following in his book, *If*:

"If you give Him complete editorial control, the Author and Finisher of our faith will write His story through your life. I can't promise a fairytale without any pain and suffering, but I can promise that it will end with happily ever after. Even better, happily forever after."[2]

There are many chapters in my life that I would have never penned myself. When God re-writes our story, we don't always understand why. We demand an explanation: "What is your logic, Lord?"

There have been many hardships in my life, but God never abandoned me. He was there before, during, and after each trial. Each hard place has a purpose whether we are privy to the final picture or not.

My dreams of happily ever after never included the following nightmares:

- Standing in a cemetery at age twelve staring blankly at a coffin that contained a huge portion of my heart descending into a grave.
- A court-delivered document with a subject line of Mr. Versus Mrs., requesting my signature that dismissed in the blink of an eye a vow that was supposed to last "for as long as you both shall live."

- My worn body collapsed in the fetal position on a cold, tile bathroom floor, doubled over in agonizing emotional pain, eyes puffy and red from the floodgate of tears with each heartbeat because the child I was carrying had none.
- Two sequels to the above.
- The loss of so many loved ones that I don't have the digits to count them.
- The current pain that is too raw to reveal, a story that I cannot allow my lips to speak and I forbid my fingers to tap out. This story too, He will work for good. Because He loves us so. His faithfulness never fails.

The One who knew me and gazed over me in the secret place of my mother's womb before anyone else had knowledge of my existence never took His hand off me even during the worst of my not so happily-ever-afters of life. He already knew, and He already knows as other conclusions are yet to be revealed. Nothing surprises Him.

These nightmares have tested and continue to test my faith. Never is it easy, but always He is there with everything He has promised. The ending is always good.

> "to bestow on them a crown of beauty
> instead of ashes,
> the oil of joy
> instead of mourning,
> and a garment of praise
> instead of a spirit of despair.
> They will be called oaks of righteousness,
> a planting of the LORD
> for the display of his splendor."
> Isaiah 61:3 (NIV)

"WHY"NING

> "Pardon me, my lord," Gideon replied, "but if the Lord is with
> us, why has all this happened to us? Where are all his won-
> ders that our ancestors told us about when they said, 'Did
> not the Lord bring us up out of Egypt?' But now the Lord has
> abandoned us and given us into the hand of Midian."
> Judges 6:13 (NIV)

The story of Gideon is full of lessons to uncover. He was called "Mighty Warrior" by God, but I used to think of him as 'wimpy warrior.' Read Judges 6 for yourself and see what you think. I now call Gideon a humble conqueror.

Do you ever find yourself asking questions like Gideon? Do you doubt God? "Excuse me, Lord, but why are you allowing this to happen?"

The Midianites had on their boots and they were walking all over the Israelites. They stole everything: cattle, sheep, donkeys, oxen, and even their land, just in time for the harvest their camels ravaged it, leaving the Israelites impoverished. They fled to hide from the invaders.

Gideon was found in the wine press threshing wheat when the Angel of the Lord appeared and seemed to have a why of His own. The angel reminded Gideon of who he was, a child of the Most High. "Oh, mighty warrior", he was called.

Gideon was in a season of sifting when he called out to God to demonstrate His power and wanted Him to move miracu-lously for him as He had moved for his ancestors.

Gideon was allowing the enemy to steal what was right-fully his and we do the same thing don't we? Instead of recog-nizing who we are in Christ, we hide and wallow in our whys and doubt God instead of girding up and facing the battle with the Power within us that only knows victory, trusting God, step-by-step.

God allows hard stuff in our lives and we cry, shout, or often scream out in anger a series of whys: Why, God? Why me? Why her? Why him? Why now? Why not?

Many times, I have answered my own cries of hopelessness with the assumptions that some measures were taken in my life because of the ugly truth of my past sin-filled life. Did my past sins cause me to relinquish my dreams and desires? The answers to both the assumptions and the questions can be, "yes and no." Yes, there are consequences to our sin; but He is a compassionate God who Redeems and Restores. I bow no longer in shame but in absolute awe of His goodness.

Sometimes, the answers are exposed with God's truth ever so gently and revealed over time as I peel back layers of anger, guilt, and shame. And honestly, there are some heartbreaks so devastating that it is beyond my intellectual capacity to comprehend why a loving God would allow them.

I am learning to trust God in all circumstances. After fits of rages, frenzies, and pouting, eventually I can collect my turbulent thoughts and thank God for the good that comes from the bad and even the ugliest of events. He is good. Always. Our immediate circumstances are visible to us in a snapshot, but God sees the whole picture. He has the supreme view.

When my daddy died of a heart attack at age 41, my young, emotionally-wrecked self, had tunnel vision and could only focus on all that our family had lost. My thoughts and concerns were all about myself and the fact that I would have to live the rest of my earthly life without my daddy. The dreams that I had planned would never materialize into memories. They vanished with his last heartbeat.

Daddy's arms would not be there waiting to embrace me through the messy years of middle school, there would be no broad shoulder to cry on and no wisdom from him to help me answer life's hardest questions.

He would not be in the stadium stands, clapping and whistling louder than any other daddy as I cheered on the Mustangs and the Hawks, or as I walked across stages to receive my diplomas.

He would never meet my beaus at the door, escort them to sit with him for a few minutes for a pop quiz, leaving them with sweaty palms and shaking knees before they escorted his princess for pizza and a movie.

The dream of him seeing me in my beautiful white gown, walking me down the aisle with tears streaming down his face, pulling back my veil on my wedding day to kiss my cheek would never come to be. The answer to, "Who gives this woman in marriage" would not be pronounced from his lips.

He would never meet my children-his grandchildren. They would never know the infectious sound of his laughter or see his big brown eyes light up when we entered the room. They would never experience his playful, adventurous, and daring spirit. He would have been their chief partner in crime.

My brothers have shipwrecked visions of their own.

And my sweet, sweet mother has lived forty-two years without her first and one true love by her side.

Thanks for tagging along on my sympathy slide. There are days I continue to grieve, not only the loss of my daddy physically, but the loss of my life plan without him. We all have reasons to grieve, whether in the palpable loss of a loved one, or a demise that is less destructive on your heart. Allowing yourself to mourn and grieve is a process that is necessary to allow our hearts to heal. There is always a turning point from this pining path to a highway of hope.

The hope implanted in my heart regarding the story of my daddy is that forty-two years later, people continue to tell me what a good man my daddy was, and they tell me incredible stories of how he touched their lives. His deeds were good, his laughter filled a room, and he loved deeply. He loved God, he loved my mama, he loved his family, and he loved others.

My daddy touched many lives in the short forty-one years he had on this earth and I believe that his sudden death from an arrested heart may have arrested others' hearts for Christ. That is my hope and that is the God-sized picture I choose to see.

"And we boast in the hope of the glory of God. Not only so, but we also glory in our sufferings, because we know that suffering produces perseverance; perseverance, character; and character, hope. And hope does not put us to shame, because God's love has been poured out into our hearts through the Holy Spirit, who has been given to us."
Romans 5:3-5 (NIV)

ASK THE GIRL IN THE MIRROR

"Wait for the Lord;
be strong and take heart
and wait for the Lord."
Psalm 27:14 (NIV)

Why did I rush ahead of God? Why didn't I listen for His direction? Why did I think I had it all figured out on my own? Why do I try to take control when I know that Your plan is best for me?

My twenties slipped away quickly, and I had slipped away from God during those years. Mired in muck, I tried desperately to fill an empty void in my life that only One can fill. I frequented bars filled with singing, dancing, laughter and booze, but the next day my soul was filled with the poisons of hangover, guilt, and shame. The embrace of men provided a false sense of security that only the embrace of my Father can provide. I'm not proud of my partying days and promiscuity, but I am so incredibly thankful for God's loving forgiveness, mercy, and grace. Through the years, I've learned to bow, no longer in shame, but in awe of what He did for me.

As I approached the ripe old age of thirty, it seemed that Prince Charming would never show up. Every day, the biological clock's tick threatened to detonate the grenade and annihilate every shred of hope for me to be a happy mother of children.

One day, a friend of mine asked if I would be interested in meeting this guy she had met through work. She chattered away about how he was tall, dark, and handsome, a bit older (although I would later find out, not necessarily wiser), was established in a good job with good pay, and came from a great family.

"What do you think?" she asked as I stood staring blankly ahead already planning what to wear on our first date. She seized me at tall, dark, and handsome.

Our courtship was careless, and we became engaged within a few months. Although I said an obligatory prayer asking for God's blessing, the fact of the folly of my flesh was that there was no stopping me from sprinting down the aisle to finally achieve the first step in fulfilling my dream. My fairytale wedding was already being planned and my life plan was falling into place. Oh, if I could go back and talk to that naïve young woman and shove her to fall on her knees before her Prince instead of sprinting down the aisle to her fabricated Prince Charming.

Three years into our marriage, and I use the term marriage loosely during this phase of my life, I discovered that the man I married was chasing a life-threatening drug for brief moments of euphoria instead of chasing life-fulfilling dreams that we had planned "for as long as you both shall live." After many years of inpatient and outpatient treatment centers, a half-way house, and many interventions from professionals and those who loved him, he continued to be deceived ruthlessly and seemed hopeless to overcome the unyielding beast of addiction.

Each day, my thoughts were filled with worry about where he was and if death had won. If I happened to find a moment of blissful forgetfulness from the reality of my life, the phone would ring and the message would quickly return my thoughts to the present: threats from drug dealers demanding their money, concerns from friends and family offering prayers for his recovery, our mothers desperately needing to hear that we were okay.

I refused to leave our home, a beautiful house that we had planned and built together. Unfortunately, the foundation on which it was fabricated was not firm. The solid Rock was not invited to bless it when we built it.

Each night, I would sleep with my bible on my pillow, opened to the pages of Psalm 91. I sense that my faceprint is there and I am certain on those pages you will find forensics of my tear stains.

Psalm 91

[1] Whoever dwells in the shelter of the Most High

will rest in the shadow of the Almighty.[a]
²I will say of the LORD, "He is my refuge and my fortress,
my God, in whom I trust."
³Surely he will save you
from the fowler's snare
and from the deadly pestilence.
⁴He will cover you with his feathers,
and under his wings you will find refuge;
his faithfulness will be your shield and rampart.
You will not fear the terror of night,
nor the arrow that flies by day,
⁶nor the pestilence that stalks in the darkness,
nor the plague that destroys at midday.
⁷A thousand may fall at your side,
ten thousand at your right hand,
but it will not come near you.
⁸You will only observe with your eyes
and see the punishment of the wicked.
⁹If you say, "The LORD is my refuge,"
and you make the Most High your dwelling,
¹⁰no harm will overtake you,
no disaster will come near your tent.
¹¹For he will command his angels concerning you
to guard you in all your ways;
¹²they will lift you up in their hands,
so that you will not strike your foot against a stone.
¹³You will tread on the lion and the cobra;
you will trample the great lion and the serpent.
¹⁴"Because he[b] loves me," says the LORD, "I will rescue him;
I will protect him, for he acknowledges my name.
¹⁵He will call on me, and I will answer him;
I will be with him in trouble,

I will deliver him and honor him.
[16] With long life I will satisfy him
and show him my salvation." (NIV)

Each morning, I crept down the stairs of our house with shaking knees to face the unknown, clinging desperately to the handrail to keep from falling or stumbling over all the rubble of shame. Pressing on toward anything normal to disguise the worry, anxiety, depression and shame that had invaded my world. Misery, fear and glum was not part of *my* plan. Definitely *not* how I would have written the story.

One day, I fell onto those shaking knees at the feet of the only One who could help me to stand back on my own. It was there that I found rest, protection, and peace. It was there I vowed to hold fast to Him and to His Word. And it was there I heard Him whisper ever so gently, "My plans for you are to prosper you and not to bring harm to you but plans for hope and a future" (Jer. 29:11).

So be it. There was hope and there is hope. In the then and there, the here and now, and the time to come. God's plan is always better than anything we could ever imagine for ourselves.

My prince charming failed me miserably, but my Prince of Peace was faithful, is faithful, and will forevermore be faithful. In that Truth, I am filled with delight.

God chose to not immediately heal the man to whom I was married from his addiction. I believe that He could have healed him in an instant, but we both had much to learn and God chose to involve us in our own victories. That thirty-something year old girl had much to learn about life and love and the desires of her heart.

Honestly, I can look back on those days and find joy. Not the kind of joy I would have recognized at the time, and not joy in the circumstances, but an indescribable joy that is rooted in God alone. A joy that comes from lessons learned, taught by the Master himself, while in the inevitable valleys we must walk.

Psalm 23, penned by King David during a period of doom and gloom for him, is one of the most inspiring and most memorized scriptures. Do we recite it so monotonously that we forget the depth of its meaning?

The Lord is my shepherd; I shall not want.
2 He maketh me to lie down in green pastures: he leadeth me beside the still waters.
3 He restoreth my soul: he leadeth me in the paths of righteousness for his name's sake.
4 Yea, though I walk through the valley of the shadow of death, I will fear no evil: for thou art with me; thy rod and thy staff they comfort me.
5 Thou preparest a table before me in the presence of mine enemies: thou anointest my head with oil; my cup runneth over.
6 Surely goodness and mercy shall follow me all the days of my life: and I will dwell in the house of the Lord forever. (KJV)

God may lead us to a valley, but He doesn't leave us there alone. He is there with us to teach, guide, direct, and prepare us for the next mountain peak. We don't always understand the reason for the ravine, but if we open our hearts and minds to learning the lessons God wants to teach us while we are there, our vision and our purpose is clear and focused as we begin to comprehend how much He desires for us to know Him, the more we want to know Him. Our most valuable lessons can be learned in the valley.

If you are in the middle of chaos, peril, sickness, distress, whatever "shadow of death" you may be experiencing, wherever there is a shadow, there is light. The light is Jesus. Never are you alone. He guides. He leads. He protects. He restores. He comforts. You will never see His back. His arms are always open and ready to embrace. We can say as "surely" as King David. Can you delight in that, my friend?

Today, when I look in the mirror, I see a woman who continues to grow in love, faith, and knowledge. I pray that my faith will continue to bloom under daily pressures and that a beautiful fragrance from those blossoms will infuse those around me and fill them with hope to help them as they persevere in their own personal battles.

"Don't run from tests and hardships, brothers and sisters. As difficult as they are, you will ultimately find joy in them; if you embrace them, your faith will blossom under pressure and teach you true patience as you endure. And true patience brought on by endurance will equip you to complete the long journey and cross the finish line-mature, complete, and wanting nothing."
James 1:2-4 (The Voice)

WAVES OF HOPE

One day, in my mid-thirties, I was lying in the fetal position on my couch in a heap of self-pity, curled underneath a blanket trying to hide the huge "D" I felt tattooed on my forehead and trying to muster up some glimpse of hope for a future, is marked in my memory. I was divorced with a slim desire to marry again. The once-strong, beaming light of desire to be a mother had flickered down to a faint glimmer of hope, and darkness was on the horizon.

I wanted to cling to hope, but the toxic memories of my past had seeped into my soul and my grip on hope had weakened. My future seemed dim. Suddenly, I remembered a tape my mama had sent to me by Charles Stanley. For reasons beyond my understanding, I couldn't swerve the urge to watch it, so I dusted it off and popped it into the VCR.

The teaching was on hope. The main character was Hannah. There is much to be learned from Hannah's story. The story was a reminder of what I already knew in my heart, but I'm not exactly a quick study as you have learned by now.

> "The account of Hannah's life in 1 Samuel 1 reveals the constant sorrow and trouble she endured. She is described as without child, downhearted, continually provoked by a rival, bitter in soul, misunderstood, and accused. Yet we discover she did not lose her grasp on hope. What was her secret?
>
> Prayer was a regular part of her life. Hannah never stopped talking things over with her heavenly Father and listening to His hopeful words. Great faith sustained her. Because of her faith, she held onto God even in bitterness of soul. By clinging to Him, she held onto her hope. She determined to persevere in prayer and faith. No matter how hard life became or how long her difficulty lasted, she continued to pray and worship God, seeking Him for the

solution. She had a spirit of sacrifice. She was willing to do whatever the Lord asked in order to make her hope a reality. With that in mind, she vowed to return her firstborn to God-the child for whom she had yearned and prayed."[3]

Hearing the story of Hannah moved me from the fetal position on my couch and on to the floor in a fetal position of prayer. By clinging once again to my Savior instead of my circumstances, my perspective began to change. I could hear my heart beat a little more happily and rapidly as I considered my future. Not necessarily the blessings that the future would bring, but the hope of the One who could settle my heart by delighting in Him alone. Recognizing that no matter when or how God chose to answer my prayers, only He could relax my skittish soul and tame my heart to delight in Him.

I met my amazing husband, John, just a few years after that fateful day when hope was renewed. We were married a little over a year after we started dating, and just as we planned, after three months of marriage we learned that we were expecting our first child. Life was good.

The excitement of hearing our child's heartbeat for the first time had my own heart racing out of my chest. With John by my side, the ultrasound technician searched for a heart-beat from within my womb, but her silence quickly revealed the horror of my worst nightmare. I stared at the black and white monitor for what seemed to be an eternity, urging and pleading God silently to reveal a flicker of life pulsing from within the inmost of my being. But instead of witnessing the drumbeat of a tiny life I had longed to see and hear, the only sight was stillness and the only sound were words that were whispered in a cold, dark room, from a stranger bearing bleak news. "I'm so sorry," she said.

We were escorted to the doctor's office, he offered his condolences and told us what to expect in the next few weeks. He told us how common miscarriages are, told us not to give up hope and shared with us how his wife had four miscarriages before she finally gave birth to a healthy baby and pointed to the "perfect family portrait" displayed in his office showing off his beautiful family of six.

He continued to talk. I'm sure it was articulate and informative, but all I could hear was ringing in my ears. Every word was a dull roar as I stared blankly ahead, straining to focus on anything to avoid my sweet husband's eyes. How could I look at him after my body had wretchedly failed us and our first child?

The horror of that day would have two sequels with the same heart-wrenching endings that tested my faith and attempted to steal my hope.

But then, something amazing happened, and it happened rather quickly.

For years, my heart had often been pricked to pray for children around the world. Children who were being raised in orphanages. Children who had no family. Children who were thirsty and hungry. Children who were abused. Children who needed to be held and who needed to feel the love of Jesus.

This pricking was not a spur-of-the-moment nick, nor a sudden urgency to pray. I believe because I had purposed my heart to delight in God, my innermost desires were beginning to branch out from the very heart of God. You see, I was still pregnant from an imperishable seed that had been planted in my heart, not my womb. And finally, I was about to start "showing."

"For you have been born again, not of perishable seed, but of imperishable, through the living and enduring word of God."
1 Peter 1:23 (NIV)

On this specific day, as I was praying for such as these, God allowed me to experience Him in a way I never had before. His Word was quickened in my heart and resurrected my God-ordained dream. His Hand was stirring embers in my heart to start a flame I didn't even know was there. God allowed me to feel the wild beat of His heart. I could supernaturally feel His enormous love for all those children precious in His sight. He allowed me a glimpse of my future. A wave of hope crashed over me, and somehow, I knew this untamed heartbeat was just the beginning of the wildest ride of my life.

[11] "You have turned for me my mourning into dancing;
you have loosed my sackcloth
and clothed me with gladness,
[12]that my glory may sing your praise and not be silent.
O Lord my God, I will give thanks to you forever!"
Psalm 30:11-12 (ESV)

Chapter 2

HANG ON TIGHT

"So let's do it-full of belief, confident that we're presentable
inside and out. Let's keep a firm grip on the promises that
keep us going."
Hebrews 10:23 (The Message)

When asked the question, "Why adoption?" our replete
answer to this question is so much more in-depth than
words could ever describe, so we allow God's finger- painted
portrait of our unique family design answer for itself. We also
have our honest but rather abrupt answer *to the* question by
answering *with a question*: "Why wouldn't we?" Of course,
that is easy for us to say now because we are living on the
other side of the journey full of twists and turns, steep hills,
and sudden rollercoaster drops that leave your tummy wondering why you left it abandoned at the top.

We pressed through the crashing waves of fears, took the
first step of faith, and we now soak up all the rewards and
embrace the constant challenges of parenthood that have
opened our eyes and hearts to love larger than we could have
ever imagined.

DESIRE TO CREATE

The adoption of our first two boys began with our longing to build our family. The seed of adoption was planted in my heart at an early age and I truly believed that one day I would adopt children. However, my plan was to have our own biological children and then adopt. Try to envision the smile on my face and hear the chuckle in my spirit as I tap out these next five words.

But God's plan was different.

After three miscarriages and several unsuccessful inseminations I finally surrendered and trusted God to reveal the desires of my heart.

His time.

His way.

Never late.

Better than anything imagined.

The surrender was not pretty, however. I had to battle out some of my mindsets with God about biological children. I can remember shouting at God that He had placed the desire in my heart to be a mother, so why had He allowed us to lose three children and then find ourselves unable to conceive again? How could He allow such gut-wrenching pain in our lives when all we wanted was the gift of children? His gift. A family. Yes, I told Him, I want to adopt, but *first* I want to experience carrying a child and the experience of birthing a child.

The fear of never being a mother was growing, suffocating my hopes and dreams.

One day, I fell face down on the floor sobbing to the only One who could answer me and charm my fears. I muddled through words something like, "Lord, you know the desires of my heart and I believe they line up with Your heart. But whatever Your plan is for us, I know that it must be good. Because your Word says so and because you are God."

There it was again, salty tears mixed with sweet surrender. Letting it go and believing in who God is, rather than what he would or would not do.

Do you remember Shadrach, Meshach and Abednego? (Daniel 3:16-18) They knew that the God they served *could* save them from the fiery furnace, but they also knew that God *could* choose to *not* rescue them. And their faith was resigned fully in who He is and not in what He would do.

So, through eyes fogged and swollen from crying, I read Psalm 37:4 again, this time with emphasis on the beginning instruction. *"Delight yourself in the Lord,* and he will give you the desires of your heart."* The emphasis is mine, but I hope you can grasp the importance of this truth: to delight in God and who He is and what pleases him. In that moment, my heart began to beat wildly in sync with His. We took our first step of faith. The Master Weaver had already created our family. We only had to say yes, so that He could bring us together.

Desire to Make a Difference

It was not until we began the adoption process that our awareness of children all over the world in need of a family to love them and care for them invaded our hearts. We began to see God at work bringing beauty to the barren. God wrecked our lives for the Fatherless. Our eyes were opened to see beyond the white picket fence in my dreams, beyond anything of such beauty and fulfillment we could have ever imagined.

We were home and settled after the Russian court judge declared us a forever family. Now, I use the term settled hesitantly. We were "settled" as much as two adults who flew across the ocean twice to bring home two toddlers who were into everything could be settled. Just sayin' folks, our world was turned upside down, but in a blissful, topsy-turvy sort of way. The youngest members were like two little hurricanes running through the house, constantly on the go and exploring every-thing, while the older two were exhausted from the challenges of instant parenthood. My immaculately cleaned house days were over and our days of snuggling with two became snug-gling with four. There was chaos and laughter. My heart was so full of joy I thought it might just explode. And my prayers of thanksgiving when I lay my head on my pillow at night had never held so much meaning. In the chaos of my world joyfully turned upside down, my heart was settled.

> "He **settles** the childless woman in her home as a happy
> mother of children. Praise the Lord."
> Psalm 113:9 (NIV)

We began attending adoption seminars to share our story with others, to raise awareness and hopefully stir the hearts of others. At one of the seminars, there was a family who had adopted a "special needs" child from China. My mind and my heart were overwhelmed at the needs of these chil-dren and the thought that they were the "least to be consid-ered" for adoption, well it simply broke my heart. I knew that I had to do something, and so I did the only thing I knew to do, which was pray.

Perusing the adoption websites specifically for the "waiting children" and praying over these beautiful beings was the least I could do. Then one day, there was one little boy who immedi-ately caught my eye and captured my heart. His eye was bright, and his cheek was rosy. No typos there. Singular.

He had a second eye, but it did not shine so brightly. The lower lid was flipped outward due a reconstructive effort to fill in his missing cheek bone underneath. My fingers are mute to type any words to describe the fervent strike in my spirit when I saw him.

Even after I closed the website page, his face was permanently imprinted in my mind. When I closed my eyes at night, it was his precious face that I saw. I printed his picture off the site and placed it on our refrigerator door and our family prayed for "Josiah to find a mama and papa to love him and help him get the medical attention he needs." Little did I know that Josiah would be our third son, and my vocal cords are not strong enough to shout to the world how thankful I am that we said yes, again, to God.

People often tell us how blessed our children are that we adopted them. Those are sweet words, but my immediate response is that John and I are the ones who are most blessed. I thank God that I may never know the desolate future we may have rescued them from, and thank God I will always know the selfish life, through them, He rescued me.

Everyone is not called to adopt, but I believe that everyone is called to help.

How, you ask? We can't do everything, but each of us can do something.

Allow me to wave the flag for you. The race has already started, but you can join in at any time. Every child has a natural God-given right to be part of a family that loves them. There are barriers along the way, but together we can break them down and empty the orphan beds.

- Prayer is a good place to start. Commit to praying for the orphans, their caregivers, and for couples who have said yes and are waiting to be joined with their child(ren).

- Pray for the people in organizations and agencies who work tirelessly each day to bring families together.
- Pray for those who have a desire to adopt but continue to allow fear to paralyze them.
- Offer your resources. You can support a family financially who are in the process of adopting. There are many organizations who can help.
- Read *and* act on what God says about the orphan.

"He ensures that orphans and widows receive justice. He shows love to the foreigners living among you and gives them food and clothing."
Deuteronomy 10:18

"But you, God, see the trouble of the afflicted. You consider their grief and take it in hand. The victims commit themselves to you; you are the helper of the fatherless."
Psalm 10:14

"And the Levite, because he has no portion or inheritance with you, and the sojourner, the fatherless, and the widow, who are within your towns, shall come and eat and be filled, that the Lord your God may bless you in all the work of your hands that you do."
Deuteronomy 14:29

"Religion that is pure and undefiled before God, the Father, is this: to visit orphans and widows in their affliction, and to keep oneself unstained from the world."
James 1:27

DESIRE TO PLEASE GOD

Don't you see that children are God's best gift?
the fruit of the womb his generous legacy?
Like a warrior's fistful of arrows
are the children of a vigorous youth.
Oh, how blessed are you parents,
with your quivers full of children!
Your enemies don't stand a chance against you;
you'll sweep them right off your doorstep."
Psalm 127:3-5 The Message (MSG)[3]

I enjoy giving thoughtful gifts. Gift cards have become a great way to give a gift to someone if we have not spent much time with them or maybe are clueless as to what they might enjoy, but for those near and dear to me, much thought is placed in the details of each gift because I want to give the person something that will put a smile on their face and make them feel extra special. Sometimes I spend hours trying to find the perfect gift.

My father-in-law is hard to buy for because he has everything, but he is always so excited about what we give him. I remember giving him a belt one Christmas because it was what he said he needed most. A brown belt was on his wish list. Really? Now a belt, a man's belt at least, seems to me such a boring gift so I was not overly excited about getting him one for Christmas. Kind of like a tie on Father's Day, you know? But when he opened that gift, jumped up, and exclaimed, "A new belt!" and whipped off his old belt to replace it with the new one, I knew we had made the right choice. He was a happy man, and everyone in the room was captivated by his excitement. Over a brown belt, for crying out loud. This man knows how to receive a gift. And he doesn't move on to open the next gift until he has properly thanked the gift giver with a hug, a kiss, and a genuine thank you.

Once, he may have had a splash too much of the good stuff and got a splash too excited about a specially designed wine glass that had been given to him for his birthday. When he placed it on the table (not so gently) to give hugs for it, he broke the stem of the glass. Thank goodness someone caught the moment on camera! His elongated face with his eyes wide open and his mouth forming a perfect "O" as he stared at the broken glass with the look of a mischievous child was captured in print for years to come. Our family continues to laugh about his detrimental excitement, but it warms my heart to know how much he appreciates his gifts. The joy of the giver is always matched with the joy of the receiver when we give my father-in-law gifts.

Occasionally, a person may take the gift that I have carefully wrapped and say thank you without opening the package in my presence. That just zaps the happy out of my giving. Part of the joy of giving the gift is watching the person unwrap it with my hope that they will be pleased with what they find. This brings me great satisfaction.

Imagine God's disappointment when we leave His gifts wrapped, maybe admiring the package from afar, but never opening the gift to enjoy.

This story of "Mr. Jones Goes to Heaven" from Bruce Wilkinson's, *The Prayer of Jabez*, benefited me in believing that God wants to bless me. He wants to bless you. He delights in blessing us with His gifts.

"There's a little fable about a Mr. Jones who dies and goes to heaven. Peter is waiting at the gates to give him a tour. Amid the splendor of golden streets, beautiful mansions, and choirs of angels that Peter shows him, Mr. Jones notices an odd-looking building. He thinks it looks like an enormous warehouse-it has no windows and only one door. But when he asks to see inside, Peter hesitates.

"You really don't want to see what's in there," he tells the new arrival.

Why would there be any secrets in heaven? Jones wonders. What incredible surprise could be waiting for me in there? When the official tour is over, he's still wondering, so he asks again to see inside the structure. Finally, Peter relents. When the apostle opens the door, Mr. Jones almost knocks him over in his haste to enter. It turns out that the enormous building is filled with row after row of shelves, floor to ceiling, each stacked neatly with white boxes tied in red ribbons.

"These boxes all have names on them," Mr. Jones muses aloud. Then turning to Peter, he asks, "Do I have one?"

"Yes, you do." Peter tries to guide Mr. Jones back outside. "Frankly," Peter says, "if I were you..."

But Mr. Jones is already dashing toward the "J" aisle to find his box. Peter follows, shaking his head. He catches up with Mr. Jones just as he is slipping the red ribbon off his box and popping the lid. Looking inside, Jones has a moment of instant recognition and he lets out a deep sigh like the ones Peter has heard so many times before. Because there in Mr. Jones's white box are all the blessings that God wanted to give to him while he was on earth... but Mr. Jones had never asked."[4]

We may often miss the mark when selecting the perfect gift for someone, but I can guarantee that your Creator never misses the mark and gives perfect gifts that bring everlasting joy and contentment.

Don't miss your miracles.

Immobilized by Fear or Revitalized by Faith?

"There is no fear in love. But perfect love drives out fear, because fear has to do with punishment. The one who fears is not made perfect in love."
1 John 4:18

Too many times during conversations about adoption I hear the fear, and dare I lovingly say, selfishness, when people say, "We thought about adoption, but _____".

Fill in the blank with some of the below comments or replace adoption with any desire or dream and list your fears.

- I am afraid we can't afford the cost of adoption.

- I am afraid I won't love an adopted child as much as I love my biological children.
- I am afraid that my biological children won't get along with the adopted child.
- We can't afford another child.
- I am afraid my husband/wife will say no.
- We have our girl and boy, so we're good.
- If our next child is another boy, then we may adopt a girl.
- If our next child is another girl, then we may adopt a boy.
- There are too many unknowns with a child that is not biologically my own. (News flash, there are a lot of unknowns in a biological child.)
- I'm too old.

These fears and rationalizations are real. I know. Most of them invaded my mind daily during our adoption process threatening to drown my hopes. These authentic fears are certainly worth examining in greater depth, which I will do in a later chapter. But for now, allow this to sink into your heart: Our world is full of God's precious gifts, and I can only imagine that His heart breaks knowing that some never step out and trust that His gifts are good.

Selfishness can block our blessings. We can be self-satisfied with our no, or, we can be delighted and blessed beyond measure with our yes when we fill ourselves with more of Him.

> [35]"Direct me in the path of your commands,
> for there I find delight.
> [36]Turn my heart toward your statutes
> and not toward selfish gain."
> Psalm 119:35-36 (NIV)

What desires drain your heart daily and what desires fill you with hope daily? Are they wealth, possessions, a nice home, recognition, promotion, sex, food, friends, elaborate vacations, lots of stuff? Keeping up with the Jones'? Or maybe to BE the Jones'? Now I'm not saying that these are bad things to desire. Well, the sex, if it's outside of marriage; the money, if you love it too much; and well, that whole coveting thing.

Overall, I don't wager that it's wrong to want nice things. When our desires for more and more deceive us, we lose our identity of who we are and forget whose we are; and in our disoriented state, we get lost on the way to true contentment. Are our desires luring us stronger than our love for Jesus?

Do you want to be filthy rich or clean rich?

There is a scripture that just recently clicked with me and now seems crystal clear when I consider all the extra weight I carry around and helps to ease my anxiety about money. Matthew 19:24 says, "Again I tell you, it is easier for a camel to go through the eye of a needle than for someone who is rich to enter the Kingdom of God."

There is a surrounding gate in Jerusalem called "Needle's Eye." Before a camel could walk through this gate, all baggage would have to be unloaded and the camel would have to get down on its knees to get to the other side, probably with much encouragement from its owner.

God wants us to be prosperous. He wants to bless us immensely. But He doesn't want us to rely on our wealth to solve our problems and He knows that our wealth will not bring true contentment. God wants us to be dependent on Him and not our paycheck, our status in society, the size of our house, or the kind of car we drive. These are the priorities of the world, not the Kingdom of God.

When I consider all the years I spent living above my means and robbing others of meaningful blessings, it slays me. The good news is that when we flip these priorities and place our dependence on God and His Kingdom, His amazing resources are abundantly poured down on us. Our passion for God will purge our lust for other things.

Perhaps it's time for a heart check and a baggage check, and like the camels going through the Needle's Eye, it may be easier if we get down on our knees.

How do our desires measure up to things that last? How do we measure our treasure? Do we love God more than the things that lure us?

May I add that I'm viewing my own set of scales, and more often than I care to admit to you, it tips in the direction of self-gratification; because yes, I want a comfortable, inviting home, fun vacations, a boat, and (God, help me) someone to clean my house once a week. Oh, heaven! Whoever says moms don't have dangerous jobs, never took the sniff test in my house!

There are many items on my want list, but true contentment won't come from those things. So, if this message tips the scales in a direction that makes your head tilt in wonder of something more, I invite you to consider what truly brings contentment to your heart. We can resolve to be content for a little while with things or we can begin to dig deeper, beneath the surface, for the greatest of treasures that will give us contentment that will last for eternity.

"Do not store up for yourselves treasures on earth, where moth and rust destroy, and where thieves break in and steal. 20 But store up for yourselves treasures in heaven, where neither moth nor rust destroys, and where thieves do not

break in or steal; 21 for where your treasure is, there your
heart will be also."
Matthew 6:19-21 (NASB)

We all have different heartbeats, passions, desires, and
longings. As a mother of adopted children, my heart is so full
it's impossible to contain the joy. Our family has been blessed
beyond measure, and I would be remiss if I didn't share this
joy with you.

Yes, there are challenges. For parents and for children.
Some of the challenges are no different from the biological
family view, and others are a steeper climb. It. Is. Not. Easy.
Whatever the struggle, at the end of the day it doesn't matter.
Your child needs you and you will do whatever it takes to help
them overcome.

Was it easy? No.

Is it easy? Lord, have mercy on all parents. No!

Has it been the wildest and most fulfilling ride of my life?
YES! And I would do it all over again in a heartbeat. If I had
known the challenges and heartaches this journey has taken
me thus far, I might still be procrastinating on saying yes, or
maybe even running the other way; but had I known then the
joy my boys were going to release into my life, I would have
sprinted faster than Usain Bolt to start the journey sooner.

God has perfect timing, and in the chapters to come, I'll
show you a glimpse of how His magnificent fingerprints are
all over us.

"For all the promises of God find their Yes in him. That is why
it is through him that we utter our Amen to God for his glory."
2 Corinthians 1:20 (ESV)

Chapter 3

FACING FEARS WITH FEAR

"The fear of the Lord is the beginning of knowledge, but fools
despise wisdom and instruction."
Proverbs 1:7 (NIV)

S ometimes we confuse the meaning of the word fear when
we speak of "fearing the Lord." There are two Hebrew
words for fear in the Bible. The first one is pachad (pakh'-ad)
which means terror, and this is not the meaning to be used
when reading this verse. The second Hebrew word is yir'-ah
(yir-aw'). This means a reverence for God.

"The expression describes that reverential attitude or holy
fear which man, when his heart is set aright, observes
toward God."
(Matthew Henry Commentary)[5]

If we choose to look for God's hand in everything, we begin
to see our circumstances through the eyes of supreme wisdom.
We chose to search for God's supreme wisdom in every step

we took in the adoption process and strove to see His hand in our lives as we moved forward and faced our fears.

PROVISION

When John and I finally said yes to begin our adoption journey, our knees were shaking and our minds were filled with fear of the unknown. One of our greatest concerns, and a primary concern of many who consider adoption, was the cost. We had researched both domestic adoption and international adoption. International adoption has more fees involved, which is expected; but for us, we could not allow the cost to compete with where our hearts were leading us.

After submitting applications to both domestic agencies and international agencies we made our decision. Our decision was based on the values and mission of the agency, along with the testimonies of families who had brought their children home utilizing the services of this agency. We knew that this was the agency that God was leading us to use, and it just so happened that (at that time) they were only an international agency.

Early in the process, I remember seeing the outlined cost of adoption while perusing the website of our adoption agency, but evidently became temporarily oblivious to the bottom line number. It wasn't until we had made the commitment and the papers were sent to us with the breakdown of the cost that I had a breakdown of emotions.

The timing was horrific since I had just finished balancing our checkbook and the balance was bleak to say the least. I went to the mailbox and our package from the agency had arrived. My dreary turned cheery as I opened the package and my excitement escalated as I read about our journey ahead. I flipped through the file excitedly to the last page and my emotions flipped out as I read the breakdown of the costs. My eyes fell to the bottom line and my excitement plummeted. The rollercoaster ride of the adoption journey does not disappoint. There's the drop. Bye -Bye tummy!

I stared blankly at the balance in our checkbook, tormented myself for not being more diligent in savings and the war of inevitable defeat began. The sobbing was ugly. When John arrived home, he found me cross-legged on the floor surrounded by a sea of white Kleenex tissues that had wiped away tears and nose blown yuckiness from my hours of sulking in deep despair.

A woman can suffocate in a sea of despair when her dream seems unreachable, but just one step toward her vision can resuscitate the passion in her heart and propel her to sprint toward her goal.

It was time to act. Time to trample defeat with victory. I believed that God was calling us to adopt internationally, and if He called us to it, He would see us through it because He is faithful. (1 Thessalonians 5:24)

"The Lord delights in those who fear him, who put their hope in his unfailing love." Psalm 147:11 (NIV)

We chose to see past our fear of finances and to see instead God's hand in our circumstances. And He provided. God opened our eyes to what He calls "pure and faultless religion by caring for the orphan" (James 1:27) – **at all cost.**

Note: There are substantial costs associated with adoption, but there are also many resources that can help lessen the financial burden. Grants are available for many of the special needs children. Some of these resources can be found on my website: pamelanorth.com.

LOVE OTHERS

"We are often mesmerized by the rich, powerful, and beautiful people of the world. We dream of associating with them; but when we focus our attention on the fashionable people of this world, it is often at the expense of those who need it the most.
Ignoring the needy and favoring the wealthy is completely contrary to the example Jesus modeled for us while walking on earth. God often chooses those who are the poorest materially to be the richest spiritually. We should welcome everyone equally into God's kingdom, even if it means upsetting boundaries like class and race. The rule is simple: we should treat others in the same way we want to be treated. God does not play favorites, and neither should we."
James 2:8 (The Voice—Commentary)

I love children. All children. But there are some children with whom I do not want to share the same roof. And I am certain that others feel the same way about my angels.

Once we were pregnant with the anticipation of bringing home our boys who are biological brothers from Russia, I started the "what if" worries. What if these precious one- and two-year-old boys end up being holy terrors? What if they don't like us? What if they have some biological disorder that we're not able to deal with? What if I heard God wrong? What if I fail as a mother? What if we never bond with them?

Our *what if* fears could have smothered our hearts aflame. But we pressed on, trusting that God would indeed bring us together with the children He intended. We knew that God was for us and His word says in Romans 8:31, "if God is for us, who can be against us?" (NIV)

God is Love.

God is good.

God is faithful.

God is for us.

Remembering these truths helped keep our hearts on fire and our worries subdued.

As previously mentioned, there was a seed of adoption planted in my heart at an early age, but I held on tightly to the hope of having biological children first. I remember obsessing about looking into the eyes of my children and seeing John's eyes.

We had just moved to Wilmington and were in a small group at the church we were attending. There was a couple in our group who were in the process of adopting their second child. Although we came to be good friends, at the time they did not know us, nor did they know yet that we were in the beginning stages of adoption. The husband, Scott, made a comment that day that rocked me to the core and I believe it came to me straight from the voice of God to loosen my grip on how I thought things should be and to cling to Him for all that would be.

The conversation was about adoption from different countries, and though I don't remember what preceded these next few words, the words struck me like a lightning bolt. He looked directly at me as he said quite frankly, "It's so *insignificant* the color of their eyes or the color of their skin." My pining over genetics ended that day and my prayer from that point forward was that I would look into the eyes of my children and see Jesus.

If you have doubts as to whether you could love a child that is not biologically your own, I assure you the answer is YES. With every fiber of your being.

Perhaps you ask if you could love an adopted child as much as your biological children. I will share with you the words of Steven Curtis Chapman regarding the adoption of their first daughter, Shaohannah:

> *"In recent years, people have commented to us about the incredible gift we've given to Shaohannah, Stevey, and Maria by making them part of our family. Those are kind words, but the truth is that Mary Beth and I, along with our other children Emily, Caleb and Will, are the ones who have been given the gift and have experienced the miracle.*
>
> *We didn't always understand this gift. At first, we thought we were called to be simply supporters to others who would adopt. We thought we were too busy; Mary Beth was unsure she could love an adopted child as much as she loved her biological children; and our family and friends had dozens of other doubts. All of those concerns melted away in a hotel hallway in China when we were handed Shaoey. Mary Beth and I knew instantly she was our daughter, that though she had come to our family differently than our first three children, Shaohannah*

was our little girl. It was a miracle, the miracle of adoption.

Mary Beth and I have vowed to not keep quiet about this miracle and the plight of orphans. Why am I so fiery? It's because I believe adoption is my story. Our story. I was homeless, hopeless, and nameless. Then God came to me and took me in and adopted me as His son. Caring for orphans in the same way God cares for us is a privilege; it is an invitation to join God right at the center of His heart as the Father to the fatherless. It wasn't until we adopted Shaohannah that we truly grasped this realization. We saw the face of Jesus."[6]

As for our family, once again, God was faithful. When I look into the eyes of my children, I see the face of Jesus. And God even added a little genetic humor to our family portrait. Wait until you see our feet.

TEAM EFFORT

"And though a man might prevail against one who is alone, two will withstand him-a threefold cord is not quickly broken."
Ecclesiastes 4:12

Many people have told me that they would like to adopt a child, but their spouse is not on board. My advice is simple and easier said than done: you can't change your spouses' heart, but God can. My simple advice:

- Pray Scripture (out loud when possible).
- Wait patiently. That's the hardest part, but just you wait. God's got this!
- Watch God at work. His power is amazing!

This was not an issue for us. John was ready to move forward with adoption when we first spoke of the possibility. But two years after our oldest boys came home, the baby bug bit me again.

I have failed to mention that when we first started the adoption process our paperwork listed infant girl as our first preference. We both really wanted a little girl. God is filled with surprises which will brand you forever of His goodness.

At the inception of thoughts that Josiah might be ours, there was cautious excitement, and debilitating doubts were spitting on every spark of excitement when I thought of him. I needed to seriously hear from God and there was some hard-core, flat on my face praying about this child. As I often do, I joked with God and said, "God could you write this one down on paper for me? Check yes or no." And He answered me in a way that will blow your socks off. This is only a partial reveal of God's fingerprints on our lives. I didn't find out the rest of it until years later. Our God is a Mighty God.

My biggest fear in moving forward to adopt a child with special needs was doubt in myself to be the kind of mother that he needed. False humility that I would have to do it on my own. I worked full time and struggled to help meet all the needs of my family. But God knew my heart and He reminded me in such an awesome way that chill bumps surface when I remember.

After begging God for an answer, I felt led to open an old prayer journal. The page literally fell open to a journal entry dated November 4th and my prayer on that date had been for parents of children with special needs. My jaw dropped and I got chills. Whoa! Okay God, I'm listening. (I will share the prayer in a later chapter).

Imagine the moment I realized that the precious little boy, whose picture was not only plastered on our refrigerator door but also on my heart, the boy our family had prayed to find a family and doctors to help him, the boy with the twinkle in his eye and a beaming rosy cheek, who had special surgical needs beyond what I could even imagine, was our son. Fill the blue balloons. It's another boy.

We were still reeling from two little boys taking over our lives. It was all wonderful and good, but still a huge change and the challenges countless. To imagine bringing in a four-year-old to add to our five and six-year-old bundles of toddling joy was sure to leave my husband to wonder if I had totally lost my mind. And to add to the already building insanity case against me? This child had special needs. And doubt set in again.

Coincidence that I had journaled about special needs parents and found that entry on the same day I had pleaded to God, although jokingly, to put the answer on paper? I knew that I had to move forward.

Next step? Tell hubby.

Honestly, I can't remember the entire conversation with John that day. I'm pretty sure the Holy Spirit took over and spoke for me. My husband is one of the most optimistic humans on the face of the earth, but even my Polly Johnny was hesitant about this next potential adventure. We had doubts, questions and insecurities:

- How would our other two boys adjust to a younger brother?
- How would we afford this adoption? Yes, isn't it funny how even after we've seen God work in miraculous ways and shown His faithfulness that we still doubt?
- Would we be able to take care of his medical needs? How many surgeries would he need?
- What would others think and say when they see his face? Ouch, that one hurts to type out.

But my husband listened intently to how I had been praying and how I felt God had answered me, and together we decided to move forward, with trembling knees. We knew that our hearts were big enough for another child, but our bank account was not matching the size of our hearts. I promised John that we would take one step at a time, moving forward as God opened doors; and if he shut them, we would stop. But God said, "I will," so we stuck our toes in the water and the water started to part people. It was amazing.

> 2 "I will go before you
> and will level the mountains[a];
> I will break down gates of bronze
> and cut through bars of iron.
> 3I will give you hidden treasures,
> riches stored in secret places,
> so that you may know that I am the Lord,
> the God of Israel, who summons you by name."
> Isaiah 45:2-3 (NIV)

After we said yes, I received a promotion which placed us over and above the China guidelines for a family of five.

We received double adoption benefits from our place of employment.

One of my co-workers was getting married and she and her fiancé asked for donations to be made to support our adoption in lieu of wedding gifts. An amazing act of selflessness.

People came out of the woodwork to help by donating items for a fund-raising yard sale.

One day at work, a co-worker overheard me expressing my fears for fees arising and it seemed that she had walked to her office and written a check to help before I even finished my conversation.

We received an unexpected insurance check in the mail at just the right time during one phase of the process. Mountain moved.

Our Camry had a recall and we received an unexpected reimbursement check for a large amount at just the right time. Bye-bye iron gate.

We had received our travel date and I was giddy with excitement. However, there was one fear crashing my party. We were short on funds for airline tickets for our two boys to travel with us. I was adamant that they make the trip with us to China to meet their new brother and pleaded with God to pave a way for our boys to "fly the friendly skies" with us.

He did.

I expressed my anxiety on an online support group about facing the possibility of traveling without our 5 and 6 -year old sons and an angel whom I had never met, sent us a check in the mail for the exact amount needed for their airline tickets. We were amazed and filled with gratitude.

I hope I get to meet this precious person face-to-face on this earth to show her how grateful we are for her generosity, but if I don't, I'm certain to meet her in heaven. I hope in the meantime that she understands the significance that her servant heart made, lending a hand to ensure that our whole family was together when we added our youngest member to our crazy mix. The memories we made were priceless.

These are just a few of the hidden treasures God had up his sleeve. He was and is so full of blessings.

We asked. We believed. We received.

STOP WATCHING THE CLOCK

"Abraham fell face down, he laughed and said to himself,
"Will a son be born to a man a- hundred- years old? Will
Sarah bear a child at the age of ninety?"
Genesis 17:17-18

Reflecting on our adoption journey, I would be remiss if this nugget of knowledge was kept from you: Stop watching the clock!

The thought of starting a family at the ripe old age of forty made me chuckle. Not exactly roll on the floor laughing as I imagine one-hundred-year-old Abraham laughed. But today I could roll on the floor laughing at myself for putting such time constraints on God.

I now cringe when I hear even a well-meaning soul announce to a sweet hopeful person, "You're not getting any younger," or hear a young woman exclaim, "My biological clock is running out." I literally must stick my tongue to the roof of my mouth to keep it still.

I remember hearing those words and rolling my eyes when I turned my head because honestly, it's the last thing a waiting heart wants to hear. But I say these words to you wrapped in so much love and hard-earned wisdom. You are free to roll your eyes without guilt but stay tuned: "God's timing really is perfect." A delay is not a denial.

When I was pregnant the third time, it was just in time for my fortieth birthday. This was such a gift to me and I'm not sure I can describe the overwhelming feeling of peace that this pregnancy brought to me. I was unsure of what was yet to come, but I had peace. Peace beyond understanding. Of course, there was a bit of anxiousness that the pregnancy would end as the previous two had and I wondered if this might be my last chance for conception. But there was peace in knowing that even if the unthinkable happened, God would still work it all out for good that was unimaginable. God gave me this amazing 40th birthday gift. And I was thankful.

There was never a medical explanation regarding our miscarriages and there was never a reason identified as to why we were unable to conceive naturally or through artificial inseminations after our third miscarriage. John had healthy swimmers and my eggs were as numerous and youthful as those of a twenty-year old. Seemed like the perfect circumstances for unity.

Somehow, these unknown answers helped me to replace my insecurity about my age with security in my maturity. God will not take us where He wants us to go until we're ready. I needed more maturity before I could understand the significance of what He was entrusting to me. God was teaching me to trust Him and all that He had planned for us. He was teaching me to grow in Him and delight in Him.

God allowed me to start seeing our circumstances through the lens of His wisdom. While we saw a snapshot, He was painting the entire portrait. He knew three children who needed a mother and father to love them as their own. He knew our hearts. And He knew our fears.

God is Love.

God is good.

God is faithful.

God is for us.

Always.

Chapter 4

ARSENALS OF DESTRUCTION

"Don't be naive. Some people will impugn your motives, others will smear your reputation-just because you believe in me. Don't be upset when they haul you before the civil authorities. Without knowing it, they've done you-and me-a favor, given you a platform for preaching the kingdom news! And don't worry about what you'll say or how you'll say it. The right words will be there; the Spirit of your Father will supply the words."
Matthew 10:18-20 (The Message)

WORDS EXHALED IN LOVE

My prayer is that these next words will be received with grace. May I preface it to say that now, on the other side of the journey, there is reconciliation, forgiveness, acceptance and support. Love was always present. We know that the words spoken by those nearest and dearest to us were breathed out of concern and love for us. The words were spoken because of their own personal fears of the unknown.

However, this chapter cannot be omitted due to some sabotaging their plan when they surrender to words of man. My prayer is that you will have the courage and strength to persevere and surrender to Abba, Father if you know He is calling you. Wise counsel is always encouraged to make certain you have heard God correctly. Wise counsel is one of the ways He speaks to us. But sometimes, you just know when your Father has spoken.

Once we had made our decision about bringing home our third son, we were hoping for the same excitement to be shared by those closest to us. We expected some resistance, but we were totally unprepared for the degree of disfavor we received. The bleak words, even though exhaled in love, breathed doubt our way and tempted to wither our dream.

They saw obstacles. We saw deliverance.

They tasted fear. We tasted victory.

They heard the ear-piercing flatline from phobias. We heard God's thundering heartbeat of hope.

Expected squeals of excitement were replaced with numbing silence.

Expected embraces of acceptance were replaced with indifference.

Expected support for a journey that we knew would not be an easy one was abandoned at their hope that we would come to our senses and change our minds.

The excitement we were hoping for was deflated by the same fears and concerns that we had already faced and tried to conquer, but now the doubts that we thought were doused permanently were once again aflame.

We respected and trusted the advice of these people that we loved dearly. It crushed us that something so beautiful, that should have united us in this adventure of faith, was dividing us. And it caused me to doubt.

On January 16, 2007, my journal entry read:

> Lord, yesterday was a horrible day filled with doubt following the conversation that has allowed waves of doubt to enter my heart yet again. Lord, flood my memory and flush these doubts by reminding me of how we got to this place.

And immediately, he did:

- The twinkling eye, rosy cheek precious face embedded in my mind for months.
- Josiah's name and its meaning-"Jehovah has healed".
- The many scriptures You placed before me.
- Your supernatural "writing on the wall" in my journal entry from 11/4/2003.

And just as I was writing the last bullet point my eyes caught the printed quote at the bottom of the journal page from Stormie Omartian encouraging us to "turn to the expert parent of all time-our Father God" and then to this verse:

"You will not have to fight this battle. Take up your positions; stand firm and see the deliverance the Lord will give you."
2 Chronicles 20:17

Tears well up in my eyes each time I remember God's faithfulness.

Abba, Father, I thanked you on that day back in 2007 and I thank you this day and every day for giving us the strength and the courage to press on, trusting You and You alone.

NAYSAYERS

Some comments made to us when we shared our heart about our adoption journey hurt because they seemed senseless. There are so many people who are unmindful of what adoption truly means and the plight of these children. Their comments caused us to tilt our heads and ask them to repeat themselves because we must have misunderstood. Then we were immediately sorry we made this request when the double impact of their words sliced our ears again.

Words hurt.

We heard it all-some of the people were not bold enough to say to our faces-but those on the receiving end were surely bold enough to ensure our ears heard it, or we overheard ourselves in whispers behind our backs.

Many of these words continue to echo in my mind more times than I care to admit. "Sticks and stones may break my bones, but words will never hurt me" is a bold-faced lie.

Thank God for reminding me of His forgiveness so I could forgive others.

THE SNEAKY SNIPER

Shortly after we brought home our first two boys there was a mission fair at our church that we attended. As I walked around looking for a booth on adoption or an orphan ministry, I was perplexed and frustrated that I could not find one. I was giddy in sharing our story and poured out my heart's desire and my vow to help make a difference in the world by raising awareness of the orphan. Fired up and ready, I fully expected to hear an "Atta Girl!" or "How can we help?" from a woman in our church that I had always admired.

She was a tiny woman, but the massive words that shot out of her mouth were offensively powerful. My balloon of enthusiasm was popped with a curt, "Honey, you don't have to reinvent the wheel. There are plenty of organizations out there to help the orphan," followed by other words that dismissed my zeal.

Lean in closely to this wisdom, my friends. If God is stirring your heart about something you believe He wants you to do, talk to Him first and seek His direction. Yes, it is wise to seek counsel from others and it's okay to ask them to pray. Please be careful with whom you share your passion. Satan is sneaky and smart, and sometimes will use the least-expected person to twist your thoughts and detour your destiny. I heard:

- You're not needed.
- Your inarticulate voice does not matter.
- Your story does not matter.
- There are plenty of workers in this field. Don't waste your time or theirs.

Her statement was true. There are indeed many successful organizations for the plight of the orphan. But current statistics show that there are 140 million orphans in the world[7], so I conclude that "the wheel" needs help, and I am determined to devote continuous action to contribute and participate in the harvest. If the statistics are miraculously narrowed down to report only one child, then it is ONE child too many. We need to keep on working until each child has come home.

For years, I allowed her statement to influence me. I knew better and should have shut out those slandering voices. For heaven's sake, I had just followed Jesus' voice and been guided by the Holy Spirit to travel half-way across the world twice to bring home the children He so beautifully weaved into our family.

But I allowed her words to drench the spark of passion planted in my heart. There was hesitation to move forward in the orphan ministry. How could I have been so foolish as to believe that God would not want to use me to share with others something so near and dear to His heart? He would never shush me in sharing our story.

Those lies tormented me for years. Not direct lies from this person who I'm certain is clueless how her words influenced me. The lies were from Satan and I hit replay every time inspiration ignited.

My thoughts were holding me captive and paralyzed in doubt. God's Word tells us in 2 Corinthians 10:5: "We demolish arguments and every pretension that sets itself up against the knowledge of God, and we take captive every thought to make it obedient to Christ."

Finally, I took her words and my thoughts and measured them against THE Word. The following are some of the truths I found to win the battle in my mind:

I heard her say "shush."
But God's Word says, "Shout:"

> "Shout the news of his victory from sea to sea,
> Take the news of his glory to the lost,
> News of his wonders to one and all."
> Psalm 96:3 (The Message)

I heard that I was not needed.
But God's Word says:

"The harvest is plentiful, but the workers are few." Matthew 9:37 (NIV)

I heard, your words are not articulate, and no one ever listens to you.

But God's Word says:

"...don't worry about what to say or how to say it. The words
you should speak will be given to you. For at that moment, it
will not be you speaking; it will be the Spirit of your Father
speaking through you."
Matthew 10:19-20 (The Voice)

*I heard, wait until your circumstances are more favorable for
a platform.*

But God's Word says:

"My job was to plant the seed, and Apollos was called to water
it. Any growth comes from God, so the ones who water and
plant have nothing to brag about. God, who causes the growth,
is the only One who matters."

Thank you, Beth Moore, for your servant heart, and in penning the bible study, *Believing God*. This study reiterated what I
already knew but dared to believe. I am who God says I am.

"And the more thoroughly convinced we become that we are
who God says we are, the more we will begin to act like who
He says we are."[8]

Beth Moore also lovingly says, "Dear One, the time has come
to believe God. The time has come to renounce words others
have spoken over us that don't line up with the truth of God's
Word. And while we're at it, let's give others the same privilege."[9]

The Flip Side

Then there's the other side of the conversation: the words that preceded those responses of unknown motive. My words. In my fervor, I don't remember the exact words that I spoke as I was sharing my elation with others.

Sometimes our passion can be so strong that it can be perceived as obsession.

My hope is that when I speak of our story it is received in a way that does not force my opinion or crusade for the orphan on you. I share our story to teach others what God taught me and how He blessed me in the process. I share my story because, once you've touched a piece of God's heart, you want to unleash your joy to the world and hope they seize the opportunity, hold on tight, and enjoy the thrill of the ride.

But caring for the orphan is not *my* crusade. It's God's crusade. I don't want anyone to take my word for it. Take His Word for it. Here's a reminder of what God tells us:

"Defend the weak and the fatherless;
uphold the cause of the poor and the oppressed."
Psalm 82:3 (NIV)

"Religion that God our Father accepts as pure and faultless is this: to look after orphans and widows in their distress and to keep oneself from being polluted by the world.

James 1:27" (NIV)

Please don't deafen your ears.

THE DEADLIEST OF WEAPONS

"Likewise, the tongue is a small part of
the body, but it makes great boasts.
Consider what a great forest is set on
fire by a small spark."
James 3:5 (NIV)

We were in Hawaii. I had won a trip for highest sales in the region, and as a recent divorcee, I asked my mother to go with me. She was reluctant about going. She doesn't like to fly and would prefer to stay close to home. (My adventurous spirit was a gift from my daddy.) However, I finally convinced her to go with me. The 50th state. The Aloha State. The Paradise of the Pacific for heaven's sake. How many people do you know who would need to be persuaded to head to paradise?

Our first night there we were on our way to dinner and came to a crossroad. The restaurant was in a courtyard below. There were escalators. No stairs. No slide. No elevator. Escalators only. My mama has a fear of escalators and the only immediate route to the restaurant was aboard this moving staircase.

I am not proud of this moment, but as we stood there watching the crowd whiz by us, and waited for mama to muster up the courage to step onto the moving steps, I looked at her and very curtly said, "It's about time you faced this fear after all these years, now come on," and probably a few more words that I'm thankful to have actually forgotten. Not my proudest moment. And spoken to my precious mama for crying out loud.

My mama bravely stepped onto the moving staircase. We enjoyed our dinner and found an alternate route back to the hotel. Later that night, I apologized to her and she forgave me, but I've never forgotten the way I spoke to her and it's doubtful that she has forgotten, either. I never stopped to consider her fear and how difficult it was for her to be out of her comfort zone. I asked God's forgiveness for my harsh tongue and He was faithful to forgive. God turned it for good, and my not-so-adventurous mama was riding a banana boat on the waves of the Pacific by the end of the week. I have beautiful pictures of proof.

There are many times in my life that I wish I had a rewind button on both my tongue and my fingertips. Words spoken (or typed) in haste, anger, pride, ignorance, envy, or to gain attention. A loose cannon, that tongue of mine can be.

A tiny little tongue, if not trained and tamed, can cause so much destruction. I have been on the receiving end, which is hurtful. But worse, I've also been the one firing the weapon of wounding words and I am so ashamed. Retraction is not an option. Weapon fired. Damage done.

We need to know when to stick our tongues to the roofs of our mouths and we need to know when to speak and how to speak. God instructs us to edify and encourage others. Not tear others down or discourage them.

> "The soothing tongue is a tree of life,
> but a perverse tongue crushes the spirit."
> Proverbs 15:4

> "Words kill, words give life;
> they're either poison or fruit-you choose."
> Proverbs 18:21 (The Message)

How do we disarm the deadly weapon and speak life? Life and death are in the power of the tongue. Let's proclaim life for ourselves and others.

- Don't wait for the sneeze to bless others-we should pray for blessings on others each day. Ask God to bring happiness and fulfillment, for lives to be enriched with benefits and spiritual prosperity. The scriptures below give us good examples of how to bless your family, your friends, and your church family in prayer:

"The Lord bless you, and keep you [protect you, sustain you, and guard you];
The Lord make His face shine upon you [with favor],
And be gracious to you [surrounding you with lovingkindness];
The Lord lift up His countenance (face) upon you [with divine approval],
And give you peace [a tranquil heart and life]."
Numbers 23:24-26 (AMP)

"For I will pour water on the thirsty land, and streams on the dry ground; I will pour out my Spirit on your offspring, and my blessing on your descendants. They will spring up like grass in a meadow, like poplar trees by flowing streams."
Isaiah 44:3-4 (NIV)

"Oh, that you would bless me and enlarge my territory! Let your hand be with me and keep me from harm so that I will be free from pain. And God granted his request."
1 Chronicles 4:10 (NIV)

- Speak with your mouth full of thanks and not grumbling. You will be amazed at how quickly your attitude turns to gratitude.

> "Whoever desires to love life
> and see good days,
> let him keep his tongue from evil
> and his lips from speaking deceit".
> 1 Peter 3:10 (ESV)

- Ask God to help you speak words to foster and not fester.

> "May these words of my mouth and this meditation
> of my heart
> be pleasing in your sight,
> Lord, my Rock and my Redeemer."
> Psalm 19:14 (NIV)

- Encourage and edify others. Did God place someone on your heart or mind today? Reach out to them, encourage them, and offer your support. You will bless them and in turn be blessed.

> "Do not let unwholesome [foul, profane, worthless, vulgar] words ever come out of your mouth, but only such speech as is good for building up others, according to the need and the occasion, so that it will be a blessing to those who hear [you speak]."
> Ephesians 4:29 (AMP)

- Speak truth in love. Show it and tell it.

"But speaking the truth in love [in all things-both our speech and our lives expressing His truth], let us grow up in all things into Him [following His example] who is the Head-Christ."
Ephesians 4:15 (AMP)

• Know when to keep your mouth shut.

[27]"Even fools are thought wise if they keep silent,
and discerning if they hold their tongues.
[28]"The one who has knowledge uses words with restraint,
and whoever has understanding is even-tempered."
Proverbs 17:27-28

[19]"Sin is not ended by multiplying words,
but the prudent hold their tongues."
Proverbs 10:19

What is your weapon of choice? My weapon of choice is the one I want wielded at me. LOVE.

Chapter 5

GOD'S FINGERPRINTS

"For we are God's masterpiece. He has created us anew in
Christ Jesus, so we can do the good things he planned for us
long ago."
Ephesians 2:10 (NLT)

I n the years B.C. (before children), I journaled regularly. The
spiritual discipline of journaling became therapeutic for my
soul. Little did I know that this small ritual would offer huge
revelations of how God was at work in my life all along. My
journals are treasured possessions to me. They record my history with God.

We love to see God work in huge ways and I surely do love
it when God shows off His power. We should praise Him for
His power. We should praise Him for His glory (who He is). But
I think it's important to note that we should praise Him in all
things and not limit our eyes to see the big stuff only. If we
don't, we may just miss the most intimate details of our Maker
at work in our lives.

God is full of surprises, and I often ask the Holy Spirit to
send me a specific word from the Word as an answer to my

plea. Sometimes, He does and other times He reveals Himself through the words of others. Other times He is silent, and I've learned that this can be an opportunity to grow in my faith as I remember His faithfulness in the past. Even though I don't hear Him, I know he is there. God may be silent, but be assured that He is at work. And oodles of times, it's not that He is silent; the truth is that I'm not still or quiet enough to hear His whisper.

No matter how God speaks to me and no matter how profound His word strikes through my flesh, flesh leaves room for doubt. Certainly, God chuckles while shaking His head the countless times I have cried out to Him through the years, like the son's father in Mark 9:24, "Father, I do believe. Help me overcome my unbelief."

And He did. And He does. Before. During. And in the aftermath. God has allowed this doubting gal the privilege of seeing His fingerprints all over our precious family from conception, leaving no room for doubt that He was with each of us all along.

NEON LIGHTS

We had received our referral from Russia. We had been matched as prospective parents who could best meet the needs of, not one child, but two. And not a girl, but two boys. Biological brothers. The agency sent our first ultrasound. The picture took forever to appear on the computer screen, but finally, there they were. Two toddlers standing side-by-side. Twenty fingers and twenty toes. I was immediately in love.

We were ecstatic and eager to get the paperwork moving. We read through the medical history, and a pediatrician who specializes in adoption reviewed the history with us. We were at peace with saying yes to a lifetime commitment to these precious boys. We signed the referral document claiming our commitment to pursue the adoption of these two boys and prepared it for FedEx to deliver.

As I anxiously awaited the pickup, doubt intruded and interrupted my peace. The fears of the past came rushing in on my peaceful thoughts, creating waves that left me swerving with uncertainty.

These unwelcome thoughts threatened panic. Not one child, but two. Provision to travel across the world to Russia not once, but twice. Provision of finances, wisdom, strength and energy to face the challenges that surely lay ahead on this wild ride. I prayed, "Can I trust you Lord? Lord, why am I doubting again? Please give me a sign, Lord. A green light? A stop sign? Yield? Please, God! If I need to grab that package back before that FedEx guy gets here, PLEASE let me know!"

God humored me and quickly flashed a neon marquee in my thoughts so bright that I would soon recognize it as the green light for which I had just prayed. The sign didn't read, "Go," but read, "Psalm 113:9."

"What?" I said out loud.

I didn't recognize that scripture reference, but there was such an intense impression in my thoughts that I couldn't flip the pages of my bible fast enough to get the answer I was certain God was providing for me. I read these words and I was no longer in doubt.

"He settles the childless woman in her home as the happy
mother of *children*. Praise the Lord."
Psalm 113:9 (NIV) Emphasis mine.

So, I did. I praised Him for what was yet to come. I praised Him for the plural of the word child that convinced me there would be ample provision for more than one.

And thankfully, the FedEx guy wasn't frightened away by the crazy lady strutting her Praise the Lord happy dance moves as she handed him the package containing signatures to claim her destiny.

Music to My Ears

The day for which we had waited, not so patiently, had finally arrived: our court date to declare Alex and Zech our own. The journey had been laborious and extensive with an obstacle course that would challenge the greatest of warriors. My greatest challenge was the four-month wait between our first visit to Russia to meet them in November 2004 and our court-appointed date in March 2005. Without God's hand on me, I may have never survived this tortuous delay.

There were no other families within our agency that had traveled to the area in Russia, so we were limited in any information regarding expectations. Typically, you're allowed to visit the orphanage for a few hours to meet the child(ren), make a decision and sign papers. This was not a streamlined process, so each region had regulations of their own. Can you imagine my ecstatic surprise when we arrived on our first visit there in November 2004, that as we were escorted straight to the hotel our guide informed us the boys were on their way to meet us there? The guide even said that the boys were going to stay overnight with us. We were going to have two days with them! I was speechless.

And my fingers are speechless now because there are no words to adequately describe the moment that you first lay eyes on your children. When they knocked on the hotel room door, I honestly couldn't tell if it was a knock on the door or my heartbeat in my ears.

When the door opened, the nannies from the children's home coaxed them gently to hug mama and papa. They recognized us from the picture book we had sent to them, sheepishly smiled, and came to us with minimal coaxing. I cuddled and hugged them. I'm surprised my pounding heartbeat didn't frighten them to tears. I inhaled the fragrance of their hair. I kissed their cheeks and babbled, "Ya lyublyu tebya" hoping they could understand my thick southern accent telling them, "I love you" in Russian. My husband did the same. I can only explain the experience as the greatest of joys I've ever known. Pure delight!

We had two amazing days with our boys playing all sorts of silly games, blowing bubbles (which was a huge hit) and the stickers we brought them ended up covering the hotel room and us. When we arrived back in the United States, we continued to find them stuck in places that brought a smile to my face. They pounced on mama and papa, riding on shoulders and horseback around the hotel suite as if we had been together for years. There were cackles and giggles and exploring and questions asked in 2- and 3-year-old Russian babble that we attempted to answer in the limited Russian vocabulary we had learned. Beautiful memories that I treasure in my heart.

The two days ended quickly, and it was time to part. I honestly thought my heart would shatter into splinters as their car pulled away. Alex was angry and Zech was sobbing with his face pressed against the window looking back at us as if we were abandoning them. In their eyes we were, and it slayed me. It was horrible! The fate of our family-to-be was now transferred into the hands of a judge in a country other than our own. We had no idea how long the wait would be before we would see them again. One second was too long for this mama. As it turned out, it would be 10,519,200 heartbeats until we met again.

During our wait, my sweet niece Suzanne was one of our biggest supporters. She made a beautiful scrapbook from our pictures which is one of my treasures. She also made a DVD for us with the pictures and to count the number of times I watched it between November 2004 and March 2005 would be too embarrassing to admit. The music was etched into my memory and every picture was memorized. The treasured disc was a portion of my saving grace on those long nights when my mind was no longer occupied with work and *To do* items. My mind became a blank space for anguish and grief to settle in and seep into my heart. I missed our boys so much I ached. They were halfway across the world. There was no Facebook or Skype. Except for minimal and brief messages from our agency, there was no communication at all.

Suzanne gave us another gift as we waited. It was a small Christmas tree to set up in their room. Each night I would light the tree, stare at the twinkling lights and curl up next to their empty toddler beds and ask God to wrap His arms around me and stretch His arms to the other side of the world to embrace our boys at the same time. These group hugs sustained me for four long and agonizing months.

So, back to that glorious day in March 2005 that had finally arrived. It was time to make our way to board the train in Moscow for our fourteen-hour train ride to claim our boys. As I was waiting for the elevator at the Hotel Ukraine to carry us to the lobby, my thoughts shifted. I realized that the next time we set foot in this hotel we would be a family of four. Emotions swept over me: anxiousness, excitement, and yes, still fear and a bit of doubt that something could go wrong.

I whispered to God, "Lord, this is it. Our lives are about to change forever. Could you please give me peace in knowing everything is going to be okay? I want to savor every second."

The elevator doors opened, and I could not believe my ears. The Master Orchestrator and Conductor of our lives had the exact song from my "Saving Grace" DVD playing in that elevator in the Hotel Ukraine. It was the sweetest music to my ears. He heard my request and answered me. His hand was still on each of us, and His peace surrounded us as we made our way to make our family of four a reality.

A Glimpse Back to the Future

It was one of those days. An exasperating parenting day. A day that left me wondering if I was messing up my kids in an awful sort of way that could very well land them in counseling for the rest of their lives. I was failing successfully. Parenting is hard. Period. With multiple exclamation marks!!!

The tiny morsel of energy I had left at the end of that day after chasing around our boys, ages 4, 5, and 6, was expended with an angry, desperate question bellowed out to God whether I had heard Him correctly after all.

"Are you sure you didn't make a mistake, God?" my exhausted, foolish self asked. "I'm not so sure I have what it takes and I think I'm getting it all wrong."

Desperate to seek rest and find peace after my raging fit, I sought last what I should have sought first. Him. As I was searching through my bible, I found three pieces of lavender paper, worn at the edge, mindlessly shuffled from page to page for at least eight years. Forgotten until this hard, exasperating, parenting day on which I desperately needed these pages to be found.

Compelled to read what was written on those pages, I discovered more than mere words. I discovered God's fingerprints.

Soon after John and I were married, we completed a passion assessment through our home church. Shame on me that I did not date this document, but we had completed it with a group in our church in Greenville, North Carolina, so please note this assessment was completed *before* we knew the heartbreak of losing three children and *prior* to any discussion of adoption.

The purpose of the passion assessment was to help identify areas of God-given passion. It was to help identify the "where" in the question, "Where should I serve?"

As soon as I type out these next words I'm just going to have to jump up and celebrate how good, faithful, and mighty is our God.

The key verse for the passion assessment was from Psalm 37:3-5:

>³Trust in the LORD and do good;
>dwell in the land and enjoy safe pasture.
>**⁴Take delight in the LORD,**
>and he will give you the desires of your heart.
>⁵Commit your way to the LORD;
>trust in him and he will do this.

Do you remember from Chapter 2 the verse that I fell flat on my face declaring *after* the heartbreaks of losing our children? Yep, that's the one.

And it gets even better.

The first two questions and my answers on the assessment:

1. If I could snap my fingers and know that I couldn't fail, what would I do? My answer was: To start a home for unwed mothers and *orphans*.

2. At the end of my life, I'd love to be able to look back and know that I'd done something about: My answer was: Caring for *abandoned children, children born with disease, orphans*, and unchurched children.

To protect my children, I won't share their personal or medical history, although one has his written all over his face; but I can tell you that this mama, who seemed to be failing miserably on that day, heard God's voice clearly as He allowed me to look back into the future. There was no mistake. He chose me. He chose them. He chose us and He wove us together as a forever family. There are no words to describe how that humbles the essence of my being. Glory!

No Forensics Necessary

In the chapter on *Facing Fear with Fear*, I revealed how God answered my prayer by revealing an old journal entry from 2003 when I was praying over Josiah (in 2006). I had jokingly asked God to provide his answer in writing. To check yes or no. And he did, through my own handwriting as a prayer to him in 2003. It was impressed upon me to open an old journal and it fell open to an entry dated November 4, 2003 (Josiah was barely 2 months old and in foster care in China at the time of this written entry). The entry read:

"Then children were brought to him, so He might put His hands on them and pray." Matthew 19:13 (ESV)

My prayer response in my journal to this verse was:

"Lord, please help those parents of children with special needs. I pray for these and all children. God, show them your love. Show me, Lord, how I can help. Use me, Lord, to minister to them. Lord, help me to not place limitations on myself, others, or You. Please reveal options and possibilities to me and help me to know they are of You."

It was not until years after Josiah had been home and I was documenting some of our journey that the date of the journal entry stopped me in my tracks. The date of the entry had never held any significance to me, only the words I had written to God shook me to the core as I realized it was a hand-written answer, as requested, from God to my own prayer. You won't convince me that God doesn't use talking (and writing) donkeys.

But on this day, as I read my treasured journal, the date November 4, 2003 jumped off the page and my knees buckled in awe and my hands shook in praise. November 5, 2007 is the day that we signed our documents in China and Josiah became ours. Now, if you are a doubting Debbie (or Thomas) and see that there is a day difference here, let me remind you of the thirteen-hour time difference between US Eastern Standard Time and Urumqi Time in China. This mama doesn't need convincing. This documented date reveals to me what God had planned all along, signed and sealed by God's very own fingerprint.

This revelation of dates and their importance to our adoption journey timeline inspired me to search for more hidden treasures that I might have missed along the way. As I plotted our timeline, I discovered yet another date that left me in awe of the Master Weaver.

Our choice of international adoption versus domestic adoption was an easy one. We researched both, but the "Spirit of Adoption" that America World shared with us was indisputable. We knew almost immediately it was our agency of choice. At the time, they were an international agency only, so our choice was easy. And above all, my heart simply felt drawn overseas.

Our first country of choice was Vietnam. Almost to the day that our decision was made to request a little girl from Vietnam, the program was closed to US adoptions. Door closed.

"Your will be done, Lord."

Our next choice was Russia, and on January 3, 2004, my husband and I signed a Letter of Request for AWAA to consider assisting us in our adoption of a child (or children) from Russia.

On January 28, 2004, we reviewed the AWAA Russia Agreement and signed our names. And so was the beginning of home study visits, months of dossier building, notarizations, certifications, and apostilles. The thrill, and the exhaustion, of a ride like no other had begun. We hurried up to wait to see the child or children God had planned for our family.

Here is the cherished nugget I missed until years after our boys were home. You see, as we set our hearts on a path of the unknown in January 2004, we trusted in God's faithfulness to lead us to our children. Unknown to us, in a small village in Russia, were two little boys, biological brothers, ages one and two, who were admitted into a children's home on a God-stamped date in January 2004.

Are each of these discoveries coincidence? Happenstance? Fate? Or God's divine fingerprints?

No forensics necessary for me to see the revelation of details, large and small, by God's own hand. Some of the intimate details of my life, as previously revealed, may seem small to some people, but they are magnified in my eyes and reveal God's power and His glory. He cares about every detail of our lives. Open your spiritual ears. Open your spiritual eyes. Hear Him. See Him. And when He reveals Himself to you, and He will, praise Him for every detail. And while not required, but highly recommended, write it down so you, too, can remember the evidence of His Presence.

> "On my bed I remember you;
> I think of you through the watches of the night."
> Psalm 63:6 (NIV)

Chapter 6

DELIGHTING IN GOD

"Take delight in the LORD,
and he will give you the desires of your heart."
Psalm 37:4 (NIV)

G od commands us to "delight in the Lord" and we will never run out of ways to delight in Him because in Him there is a flood of fabulous joy to discover. This is not a request or a suggestion, but a directive that calls for action. Too often, we skip the instructions and skip to, "What's in it for me?" Like the offspring of leeches, Gimme! And Gimme more! (Prov. 30:15). We self-examine our hearts and see our intentions and works as good, concluding that if our desires are good, then God will graciously give us what we deserve. We have a dishonorable expectation of entitlement.

But God gives us the opposite, which is what none of us deserves. Forgiveness. Mercy. Grace. Only God can examine our hearts and He will gently show us what needs to be revealed and confessed to Him.

"Investigate my life, O God,

find out everything about me;
Cross-examine and test me,
get a clear picture of what I'm about;
See for yourself whether I've done anything wrong
then guide me on the road to eternal life."
Psalm 139:23-24 (The Message)

God instructs us to delight in Him because He knows that when we do, our souls are satisfied beyond measure. God wants us to know Him because knowing Him is how we delight in Him. As A.W. Tozer says in *Delighting in God*, "To truly know God as He desires and deserves to be known is not a casual thing, but a lifelong pursuit that ends only when we see Him face-to-face."[10]

Once we begin to know Him and grasp that He is all we need, He is all we desire to grasp. Once we begin to know God, the missile of hunger for more knowledge of Him is launched.

God desires for us to be dependent on Him. When we flip the switch in our mind to see that God's instructions guide us to map out our freedom, we recognize that following Him, loving Him, delighting in Him, and yes, obeying Him is our privilege. We get to do life with Him.

We can't delight in God, enjoy Him, and rest in Him if we are anxious, worried, and troubled. We are instructed multiple times in Psalm 37, "Do not fret." We must trust.

God instructs us to delight in Him, but God also delights in us. "You exist for his benefit, his glory, his purpose, and his delight."[11]

"For the LORD takes delight in his people;
he crowns the humble with victory."
Psalm 149:4 (NIV)

"The Lord your God is with you, the Mighty Warrior who saves. He will take great delight in you; in his love he will no longer rebuke you but will rejoice over you with singing."
Zephaniah 3:17 (NIV)

The truth that God delights in me blows my mind. There are many days my prayer is, "God, help me to see me through Your eyes, because it is hard for me to wrap my mind around the truth that You delight in me. Help me to see the master-piece you created in me, and Lord, thank you and praise You that You are not finished yet. Keep teaching me, Lord. I have so much to learn."

I've made so many mistakes in my life. I invited Jesus into my life at an early age and was baptized at the age of twelve. It was in middle school that I learned to cling to my Heavenly Father since my earthly father was no longer with me, but as I entered high school I began to fade in my faith and the thirst I once had for more knowledge of Him was pseudo-quenched by the contaminated solutions of the world. One path of dis-obedience led to many paths of destruction and foolishness. When I left home for college, I envisioned freedom, but the choices I made only led to a life imprisoned by guilt and shame.

I have grieved the Holy Spirit with my own rowdy, rebel-lious, control-freak flesh that battled to have my own way and fulfill my own pleasures. My sins separated me from God. I was desperate to fill a void that only One can fill. I was searching for who I was without recognizing Whose I was. God's stead-fast love and mercy never left me, but I was stumbling over the rubble of disgrace instead of reaching out to His hand always extended with grace.

I have found the quickest route back to the High Way after years of detouring on winding roads of destruction is on our knees. Sometimes we humble ourselves to this position and other times God buckles our knees for us. God loves me too much to allow me to stray any further. I could not recognize my Shepherd's voice because I had strayed too far from Him or perhaps chose to ignore Him. Thank God, he buckled my knees and humbled my soul. As unpleasant as it was to fall from my mountaintop of pride, as soon as He buckled my knees there was an outpouring of confessions and an overflow of love that only He could provide. Don't turn your back on God, turn to Him and turn swiftly. Change your direction and change your mind. Tell Him what He already knows. Pour out your heart to Him as He pours His love on you.

"And hope does not put us to shame, because God's love has been poured out into our hearts through the Holy Spirit, who has been given to us."
Romans 5:5 (NIV)

God doesn't drizzle His love on us. He abundantly pours out His love. His love gushes out on us. He floods our hearts with His love. Our part is somewhat simple. Open your heart, open your eyes, open your ears, open your arms to receive all the love He has to give.

"We can't round up enough containers to hold everything God generously pours into our lives through the Holy Spirit!"
Romans 5:5 (The Message)

"And hope will never fail to satisfy our deepest need because the Holy Spirit that was given to us has flooded our hearts with God's love."
Romans 5:5 (The Voice)

"Such hope [in God's promises] never disappoints *us*, because
God's love has been abundantly poured out within our
hearts through the Holy Spirit who was given to us."
Romans 5:5 (AMP)

God's love will never be in short supply. It's Who He is.
"God is Love" (1 John 4:8).

"Praise You, Lord, with all my soul, and I desire never to
forget all Your benefits-You, Lord, are the one who forgives
all my sins and heals my diseases, who redeems my life from
the pit and crowns me with love and compassion, who satisfies my desires with good things so that my youth is renewed
like the eagle's. You, Lord, work righteousness and justice for
all the oppressed."
Psalm 103:2-6 (NIV)

Can you delight in this Truth?

Praise Him

"So *let the music begin*; praise His name-dance and sing
to *the rhythm of* the tambourine, and *to the tune of*
the harp."
Psalm 149:3 (The Voice)

Merriam-Webster defines syncopation as "a temporary
displacement of the regular metrical accent in music" and
Dictionary.com defines it as "to place (the accents) on beats
that are normally unaccented." Considering the definition from
Wikipedia, syncopation is a general term for "a disturbance or
interruption of the regular flow of rhythm:" a "placement of

rhythmic stresses or accents where they wouldn't normally occur." Syncopation creates excitement and brings an unexpected playfulness to music.

If you didn't grow up in the 80's, I highly suggest you search YouTube and listen to Gloria Estefan belting out, "Turn the Beat Around." I dare you to not get up and dance.

Music is awesome and inspirational. The composition of notes threaded together connects people worldwide. Music is therapeutic. When listening ears can't understand our sorrows, music lends our ears therapy that soothes our souls. Music stirs us and compels us to sing and dance. Music moves us to tears or sparks a smile. Music motivates us to move or relaxes us to renew. Music helps us to forget our worries and helps us to remember our blessings.

The gamut for my music genres is extensive. My daddy used to wake me up in the mornings with an ear-piercing volume to the tunes of Loretta Lynn, Conway Twitty, George Jones, and Dolly Parton. I'm sure I probably rolled my eyes each morning as I crawled out of bed. I mean, what voices could start a young gal's morning better? Those memories are priceless to me. To this day, I carry on his love of early morning and his love of country music, and if I close my eyes and listen closely, I can almost hear him belting out some twangy tunes from heaven.

As a dancer, thirty years and at least thirty pounds ago, I came to appreciate classical and jazz. "I love rock and roll" as much as Joan Jett, and as a girl who grew up in the '80s, well let's just say, all music from the '80s was the best of the best. My boys roll their eyes when I start dancing to the tunes, but let's say it together, fellow '80s sojourners, "Nobody puts baby in a corner." (Dirty Dancing) They'll recover from embarrassment. I'm dancing, y'all.

But it is worship music that changes our heart for God. We can "get our worship on" with Jamie Grace or many of the other anointed Christian artists of our generation. I love to listen to praise music and dance and worship God. Growing up in a Southern Baptist church, I've finally discovered it's okay to wiggle when you worship.

But worship is not just about music. Rick Warren says in The Purpose Driven Life, "Offering yourself to God is what worship is all about."[12] Often the worship begins in silence and just being still before God. Offer yourself before Him in complete submission. Read His Word. Listen for God's voice that sometimes is channeled through an unexpected heartbeat. And as I praise and worship Him, my heart races faster, and soon it is about to explode in praise. And may I say with the utmost respect and reverence for my Heavenly Father, that "He nails that beat with the syncopated rhythm with the rat-tat-tat-tat-tat-tat on the drums..." ...of my heart. There's nothing like a heart beating in sync with God's. It's exhilarating. Pure joy. Delight.

"I delight greatly in the Lord; my soul rejoices in my God."
Isaiah 61:10 (NIV)

"I will sing for joy in God, explode in praise from deep in my soul."
Isaiah 61:10 (The Message)

Lord, please interrupt my rhythm anytime. Surprise me, Lord!

It's Personal

To delight in God and love Him, we must know Him. To know Him, we must have a personal relationship with Him. To have a personal relationship with Him, we must have communication with Him. To truly know ourselves, our purpose, and our deepest desires, we must communicate with Him on an intimate level so that He can remind us who we are and the purpose for which He created us.

It's personal, people.

A.W. Tozer states in Delighting in God, "Once you begin probing into the personality of God, there is no end in sight. It goes on and on as He delights to unfold himself before our worshipping hearts."[13] God's desire is to have a personal relationship with you and me.

Can we stop and let that truth sink into the depth of our hearts? Why wouldn't He? He sent His one and only Son to save us from our sin so that we could have eternal life in heaven with Him. That's personal. Jesus came to save us, but He also came to teach us how to live in this crazy mixed-up world and find our promised land here on earth.

As I've said before, my relationship with God began early in life, and I have experienced, and continue to experience, many detours along the way. I could have never conceived what the past twelve years have added to my life-the absolute greatest assignments of my life thus far.

It's an exhilarating and exhausting ride. Raising three boys and balancing parenting and marriage, along with working full-time, left me little time to spend with God praying and studying His Word. (I chuckle now when reading this because I have discovered that the more time we spend with God, the more He expands our time or arranges our schedules to accomplish everything we need to in the 24 hours He gives us each day). Sure, I still prayed and read Scripture, but somewhere along the way, I lost connection with Him. I could take the time to list the many reasons and excuses for not carving out more time with Him I had, but I'm sure you've already heard them all. Some of them were legitimate, but many were deceptive. Whatever the reason or excuse, the result was the same. I was desperate to reconnect with Him. Desperate to hear His voice and feel His Presence.

"The human heart has a thirst for God. God created us, and something in us relates to something in God. Until these two are brought together, which happens at salvation, there is restlessness within the human heart that can never be stilled." [12] There are droughts in my life when my heart becomes restless and my soul becomes thirsty. My knowledge of God reminds me where to find rest and Who can quench my thirst, but until I act on this knowledge, I feel trapped.

When I disappoint the people I love the most on this earth, I convince myself that I am not enough. Tugged in so many different directions to fill my roles as wife, mother, daughter, sister, friend, small-group leader, employee, and the list goes on, I feel less than enough to fill my own shoes. Maybe that's why I find freedom in going barefoot all the time.

Have you ever felt trapped in the vicious cycle of life? For years, I felt snared on a wheel that kept me running faster and harder each day and it seemed impossible to jump off for a much-needed reprieve. There were deadlines at work, appointments for my children, soccer practice, bowling league, church commitments, school events, school meetings. Date night with my husband? Um...when might we fit that in? You get the gist.

I wanted to be the best at every character my Casting Director had assigned to me. And these are all good things. My roles were assigned, and each one I am so grateful for, but I was totally botching the assignments.

My responsibilities were pulling me in countless directions and I could only run in circles. Round and round on a wheel that landed me nowhere except in an all-too-familiar territory of guilt, shame, exhaustion, and despair for being mediocre at many things but failing at doing even ONE thing well. Can you relate?

Direction for my life is what I desperately needed. Guidance. Fulfillment. What happened to my joy? I prayed daily for a way to end this cycle of defeat, but when you're running in circles, your panting makes it difficult to hear God, and even if you hear the direction you can't heed a direction to turn right or left, go straight, or simply wait. You end up right where you started.

A decision had to be made and I finally realized that to make a change I had to slow down for a long overdue retreat with my Maker. Oh, how I had missed our conversations. I desperately needed carved-out time for studying, prayer and fasting. I needed to be still to hear His voice above all the other noise in my life.

And you know, even though I couldn't hear God or feel His Presence during this drought in my life does not mean He had left me. His word promises that, "He will never leave you or forsake you." (Hebrews 13:5) Our faithful God was right there all along working everything out for good and when I was finally still enough to hear Him, He provided answers.

The revelation was to douse the worldly-born burning desire to get everything right and fan into flame the desire to do the good works that were prepared in advance for me.

(Ephesians 2:10) If I don't stop, listen, and follow through I miss the mission. The daily mission, the hourly mission, the split-second decision mission. The mission under my very own roof, in my community, my church, the world. And the thought of missing out on even ONE of these assignments ordained for me-by my Creator makes me physically ill. When my desire is to accomplish the assignments chosen for me in this "chosen generation" (1 Peter 2:9 KJV), my energy level soars to new heights and I'm ready to run the race marked out for me. (Hebrews 12:1). One delightful step, skip, or sprint at a time.

His Works

How often do you stop to savor the beauty of God's creational glory? For me, it's not often enough and it baffles me because the benefits of taking pleasure in God's creation bring me peace and humble me to a place of sincere worship.

We live near the ocean and I can have happiness scrunching my toes in the sand, inhaling salt air into my lungs, and listening to the roaring waves at any time of the day. But I must decide to pull myself away from the hustle and bustle of my day to go there. This ocean is one of my happy places where I can worship God simply by admiring the beauty of all He has created. With one glimpse of the blanket of blue or green my heart begins to worship my Creator. He paints a sunrise and sunset for us each day. Are you watching?

On some days, God surprises me with glimpses of dolphins, an unexpected shell that washes over my feet, and on one rare occasion he surprised John and me with a whale sighting. The whale was swimming slowly along the shoreline and my heart was stirred to praise God for creating such a magnificent creature.

God wants us to enjoy His creations. There are some creatures that I would never in a million years have thought would kindle an appeal to worship God, but the magnificence and detail of these creatures up close and personal caused me to recognize the beauty and uniqueness of all things created.

One of my boys has always had a fascination with snakes, and for years, as a toddler and through elementary school, the only books that he wanted to read at night were about snakes. Occasionally, I could sneak in "Charlie Caterpillar," but he always insisted on a snake book. With the accent of Kaa, from Jungle Book[14], listen as I say, "trussssssstttt me," this mama knows more about snakes than I ever wanted to know. Not exactly what I wanted to read just before settling in for the night, but I love my son. So, we read books about snakes, and have mercy, they all included pictures.

Years ago, I decided to become mother of the year and contacted our local Cape Fear Serpentarium to celebrate our boys' birthday party there. This facility is unique and recognized all over the world for over 40 venomous species of snakes, exotic lizards, iguanas and crocodiles to view. There are bushmasters, vipers, mambas, cobras, pythons and many more species. They are displayed in replicated features of natural habitat and surrounded by glass, so viewers can "safely" get up close and personal to observe their behaviors. They even allow you to watch as the brave, or out of his mind crazy, herpetologist feeds these deadly creatures. Truly, it was fascinating and exhilarating to watch.

I must admit that as we entered this brick and glass house of the venomous, my heart was racing and I declared myself a fool to escort my children and their young friends into a structure where one escapee could be hazardous for all. But as I moved along from one exhibit to another my mind began absorbing the detail and beauty of these creatures. Yes, I said beauty. I had moved past my fear, which was appropriate, long enough to appreciate the uniqueness and detail of each one, I became amazed at the works of our Creator. The colors and the intricate detail of their skin, their movement, and those dang fangs and elongated tongues. It was an amazing experience to recognize God for the amazing handiwork of all creatures great and small.

Don't get me wrong. This was not my happy place, but even amid anxiety and fear of these reptiles, God heightened my awareness of His wonders. And don't worry, I never once forgot that the ancestor of these wily creatures was front and center before the fall of man. As the Word states, "...the serpent was more crafty (subtle, skilled in deceit) than any living creature of the field which the Lord God had made" (Gen. 3:1 AMP). Yes, I was amazed, but not deceived.

If we simply take the time to notice, we can enjoy God's wonders anywhere and at any time. When is the last time you took the time to enjoy a sunrise or sunset? Stepped outside on a night filled with bright and shiny stars and breathed in the wonder of them all? Played tag with a butterfly or let a ladybug tickle your skin? Have you stopped to observe the magnificence of a spider's web? When was the last time you stopped to smell the flowers? Cliché, I know, but if it helps us to slow down, enjoy life, enjoy creation, enjoy the details and delight in God, let's do it. Freeze frame the moments in the archives of your mind. You will want to retrieve them throughout your day.

And by the way, my ssson ssstill hasss a fassscination with sssnakes. Your prayers are greatly appreciated.

CAN I TRUST YOU, LORD?

> "So do not fear, for I am with you;
> do not be dismayed, for I am your God.
> I will strengthen you and help you;
> I will uphold you with my righteous right hand."
> Isaiah 41:10 (NIV)

Daddy and I were alone in our living room. One brother had already moved out of the house, married with a family of his own, and my other brother was away at college. My mama would soon be headed to work for the graveyard shift, so she was piddling, likely cleaning before going in to work at midnight.

Daddy was rocking in his Boston Rocker, drinking an ice-cold Pepsi, and I was curled up on the couch searching through the special Christmas edition of the Sears and Roebuck catalog composing my wish list. Giddily, I announced to Daddy that I had found the perfect gift for him. I showed him a picture of a male model wearing red, silk pajamas. They were hideous. We both laughed at the thought of my country music loving, hard-working, calloused, tobacco farming, electronic engineering Daddy in red silk jammies. I put away the catalog to get ready for bed, gave him a quick goodnight hug and told him I loved him. Through the years, I have convinced myself that I told him I loved him because I can't bear the thought that my last words to him were anything other than those precious words. Not just words. Truth. I loved him so.

The next November morning in 1974, I crawled out of bed to get ready for school. I heard a buzzing noise as I walked to the bathroom, but my mind was fuzzy in my sleepy state and didn't focus on it too much. Then it occurred to me that

Daddy had not awakened me as he usually does, crooning to the tunes of George Jones or Loretta Lynn to the top of his lungs as he shaved. I turned off the water faucet to focus on what that buzzing sound was. It was the alarm clock. Why hadn't Daddy turned it off yet?

I went to his room to find him still in bed. "Daddy, it's time to get up. DADDY, get up. DADDY, GET UP!!! DADDY, PLEASE GET UP!!!"

Death seems so final for those of us left behind in our earthly home. We must live the rest of our lives here on earth without the loved ones who have gone before us. This mission seems impossible because we love so deeply. My daddy knew Jesus and is now in heaven, so life for him is eternal and I know that one day I will be with him again. But the twelve-year old girl left behind to live her life? Her life would be changed forever. And part of that life would be trying to take control of all that she could not control on that early November morning.

My daddy was someone I trusted. I knew that his strong hands would protect me and discipline me when needed. I was fearless when he was around, jumping into the deep waters of the Pamlico Sound, knowing that if I got into trouble, he was there to rescue me. I remember my first flight which was in a small engine plane, but with Daddy beside me I was confident everything would be okay. There was no rollercoaster I refused to ride if Daddy was by my side. And what beautiful sights and thrills I would have missed if I had been too afraid to say yes.

One of my favorite pictures is of me as a young toddler in my little high-top *Stride Rites* walking shoes, barely able to stand, wobbling on the top of our car. Don't judge my parents for having me on the top of our car; I don't know why I was up there, but I'm sort of certain from the look on my face that I hadn't asked to be placed up there. I'm convinced that

Daddy had a lesson in store for me, and I'm positive that my daddy took his eyes off me for only a millisecond, which is the amount of time it takes a human eye to blink.

The ground was a long way down in the eyes of a tiny toddler, but my daddy's outstretched hands offered the courage I needed. I like to imagine the banter. "Come on brown-eyed monkey. I'm right here. Go ahead and jump." Me, with furrowed brow, pursed lips and sassy little squeaky voice, "NO! I scared, Daddy." Then Daddy, "It's okay. I'm not going to let anything happen to you, trust me." I would imagine this tête-à-tête between a toddler and thirty-year old continued for a while before I mustered up the courage to leap into his arms. I can see the smile on my face as I land safely in his arms, and hear an apt, "Again, Daddy! Catch me again!"

My daddy was instilling in me the ability to trust so that I could enjoy all the amazing adventures my Heavenly Father had planned for me, if only I would trust Him and jump into His plan.

God repeats to us in His Word to not fear. The bible is filled with great stories of celebrated men and women that feared when God called them to "jump" into an adventure with Him:

- Moses cried out, "Who am I?" And God said, "I will help you" (Exod. 3:11, 4:12).
- Gideon made excuses, "How can I, I am weak?" And God replied, "I will be with you" (Judg. 6:15).
- Jeremiah resisted, "I can't speak;" "I am too young." And God said, "Do not be afraid... I am with you and will rescue you" (Jer. 1:6).

God is with us and He rescues us, which lets me know there will be times I will be in deep waters. I must trust and remember.

Jesus is the name I was introduced to from the very beginning of my life. I was taught about His love-that He is Love
(1 John 4:8). My parents took me to church on Sunday. I was
involved in youth group and sang in the youth choir. I learned
about Jesus from my parents, grandparents, aunts and uncles,
Sunday school teachers, pastors, Billy Graham's television
broadcast, and a soul-winning cousin two years my senior.
Many people helped to instill God's truth into my life.

But how can I trust God in a devastating loss that I couldn't
even comprehend in my twelve-year old mind until many years
later? Even though my heart was broken and I couldn't understand why such a loving God would allow my daddy to die,
I believed that Jesus still loved me. Through the years after
losing Daddy, I chose to believe that God is fair, loving, and
merciful and must remember that His ways are not our ways
and we won't always understand them (Isaiah 44:8). I chose
to believe that He took a huge piece of my heart, but He continues to fill it with vast volumes of love every day.

He never left me. He still protects me. He loves me, and the
thrill of the ride with Him by my side, I am hopeless to expound.

"Start a child off in the way they should go and even when
they are old they will not turn from it."
Proverbs 22:6

The way we get there is different for each of us, but there
is only One Way to eternal life. Some of us are brought up
in Christian homes and learn about the love of God early
on. Many friends of mine were not brought up in Christian
homes but learned later in life about Jesus and His love for
them. And yes, there are some who were indeed brought up in

Christian homes, taught early on about Jesus and still choose their own way.

Jesus tells us in John 14:6, "I am the way, the truth and the life. No one comes to the Father except through me."

My head was filled from what I was being taught at home, in church service, and in Sunday school. I had much head knowledge of what being a Christian was supposed to be like. Head knowledge is good and much needed as we grow and learn. But heart knowledge is a revelation that you just know as it is revealed by the Holy Spirit to our minds and to our spirits.

What I knew, alone, did not give me the ability to truly trust Him. I needed to taste His goodness. I can read and find out all the facts about honey and know it is sweet, but until I taste it, I won't truly know its satisfying sweetness.

"Oh, taste and see that the Lord is good! Blessed is the man who takes refuge in him!"
Psalm 34:8 (ESV)

We are instructed to "commit our way to the Lord." The more we know Him, the more we know we can trust Him, and when we trust Him, we are committed to His ways. It's tough to trust God when your heart is broken over something that seems as senseless as a life taken too soon. Paul says in Romans 8:28, "And we know that in all things God works for the good of those who love him, who have been called according to his purpose."

"All things? Even death and wicked events that happen to good people? IT'S NOT FAIR," we scream.

My relationship with Jesus is how I know that He is good. I choose to believe Romans 8:28 and Genesis 50:20, "You intended to harm me, but God intended it for good to accomplish what is now being done, the saving of many lives."

I will never know until I can ask Him face-to-face the reason my daddy had to die at such an early age leaving me, my mother, and my brothers to exist in a world without him. Yes, he made poor choices regarding his health by smoking, but so do many people who live longer lives. For now, I continue to trust what I have learned and what I have grown to know. God is good. God is faithful. God is love.

OBEDIENCE-OUCH!

My mama has the disciplining "Evil Eva Eyes" as we call them. Those eyes could cut like a knife when we were out of line. No need for a talkin' to or a spanking. Those eyes said it all. They still can, and we, children and grandchildren alike, occasionally receive the look that slices through our nonsense.

There were only a few spankings in my childhood from my daddy that I remember, but I deserved each of them. As a parent, I recognize this discipline as a vital act of love. To guide and direct us on a path that is safe. Three of my spankings were because I had "gone astray." Three. Yep! Stubborn.

Without our parent's knowledge, my cousins and I strayed off into the woods while our frantic parents, aunts, and uncles searched for us. We strayed off into the canal on a paddle boat, without our parent's knowledge, where we got stuck up to our eyeballs in muck until the tide came back in. Meanwhile, my mama was screaming up and down the dirt road parallel to the canal, petrified that we had drowned.

Another time I strayed off to a neighbor's house, without my parent's knowledge, and still wasn't home by curfew. I can recollect the dread I felt in the pit of my stomach before walking through the door because I knew I was late, and I knew they were worried about me.

Not the brightest kid on the block.

And I knew what was coming. I had disobeyed and there were consequences.

Obeying is important. And if it's someone we trust and love, we should recognize that obedience is for our own good. We may not recognize it in the heat of the moment, but eventually we know it was for our own good.

Maybe I learned my lesson where my parents were concerned, and I finally learned that I had better let them know my whereabouts and be home at the time I was supposed to be home.

With God, I continued to stray. I still continue to stray. God tells us to obey Him, yet I continue to try it my own way. Why? Darn that fickle flesh.

Praise God that our distance from Him does not change His love for us.

Bruce Wilkinson says in *Secrets of The Vine-Breaking Through to Abundance*, "Responding to God's discipline brings immediate benefits. When we allow discipline to train us, we not only escape our sin, but we also grow in maturity. Hebrews 12:11, talks about the "peaceable fruit of righteousness for those who have been trained by it." Repentance doesn't just get us back to zero-God takes us from a minus ten to a plus ten. Neither is repentance a one-time act. It is a lifestyle, an ongoing commitment to keep putting aside our rebellion and receive God's forgiveness."[15]

We never lose when we are obedient to God. It takes strength to say no to certain circumstances that we know are sinful. There are consequences to sin and we need strength to battle out the temptation. Please know that God never tempts us, He only tests us. The temptation comes from Satan. Strength for the battle comes from God.

The story of Joseph and Potiphar's wife is a good example of sensual temptation and the strength Joseph had to say no to her. Read Genesis 3 to get the whole scandalous story. To summarize, Potiphar's wife tried to seduce Joseph, not once but day after day. Joseph said to her, "How could I do such a wicked thing and sin against God?" (Genesis 3:9) Potiphar's wife was rejected, angry, and tricked others into thinking Joseph tried to attack her and Joseph was imprisoned. There is a lot more to the spicy story so be sure to read it. Spoiler alert (in case you don't know the story), Joseph eventually became ruler over all of Egypt. Obedience brings blessings.

Whatever the temptation: sexual, financial, or opportunity, we need to discipline ourselves and ask God daily to give us the strength to say no.

Use the acronym: S.T.O.P

S – *Stop* to think of the costs. Your purity, integrity, and honesty to name a few. Is it worth it?

T – *Think* about why you are even considering moving forward with something you know is wrong and will lead to disaster. Fear of rejection, the loss of a relationship, a loss of financial opportunity are strong emotions. This kind of fear is a liar.

O – *Obey* God. Trust Him. He will lead you exactly where He wants you to be and bless you beyond measure.

P – *Praise* Him for helping you to obey Him.

Don't be defiant and block your own blessings. Be compliant and your blessings will be countless.

THOU SHALT KNOTS

When you think of the story of the Ten Commandments, what is the picture in your mind? My thoughts used to be that of a Mighty Thundering Voice that boomed out from billows of smoke and ordered us to follow these rules or the jagged lightning bolt that accompanied the thunder would strike me dead. But God knows us, and yes, these are commandments and we should obey them. However, just like those humans on the Mount who broke at least two of the commandments before they got to the bottom of the mountain, He knew we couldn't keep them on our own. We need Him.

God gave us a Top 10 list of "Thou Shalt Nots" and I sometimes I forget about this treasured tablet of wisdom. Most of them I foolishly consider easy A's, but those bookends are two that God has made me more aware of recently, and together, they are often the culprit of my fluttering feeling of discontentment.

Exodus 20:3 "You shall have no other gods before me." (NIV)

Exodus 20:17 "You shall not covet your neighbor's house; you shall not covet your neighbor's wife, or his male servant, or his female servant, or his ox, or his donkey, or anything that is your neighbor's." (NIV)

My mind is a scary place and there are some grave lies that take up residence there. When I think about the 10 commandments, I rank myself as passing:

- I don't worship idols. At least not those shiny little statues that come forth in my shallow thoughts of the word, idol. What about those things that distract me and keep me from spending time with God? Idols (anything that stands between you and God) are usually subtle. For example, do you check in with God first thing in the morning or check on emails or social media? Before I know it, the first 30 minutes of my day has passed me by without praising the One who created me and asking Him to guide my day.

- I don't swear using God's name. Then I started digging deeper and had to put the shovel aside because I am so guilty of tossing His name around disrespectfully.
- I love and honor my mama and my husband's parents. Well, love, yes. Honor them? I'm hesitant to profess victory on honor.
- I don't lie, cheat or steal. Does copying personal items at work count? Or what about all those pens from work that end up in the bottom of my purse-the good writing ones. Hmmm?
- I don't bear false witness against my neighbor. Unless I consider the instances when I falsely accuse one child, solely on actions of his past, of wrongdoing before hearing all sides of the story.
- I have never murdered. Although, if you hurt my husband, our children, or my mama, I may consider the thought.
- I am faithful to my husband, except when I watch too many Hallmark movies and start living in a fantasy of perfection.
- I cherish God's gift of rest on whatever day my Sabbath falls and sometimes my lazy self steals an extra one.

For most of my life, I have skimmed over these commandments without digging into them and finding the beautiful treasures God has written out for us. Instead of the thundering voice of disappointment from God as I fail in these categories, the picture in my mind now shows God bending down and whispering in my ear, "If you follow these instructions that I put into place for you, our relationship will grow and flourish. That is my desire. What about yours?" Exodus 20 starts off, "I am the Lord your God." It's not about legalism; it's about relationship. He is my God. He is Your God. He is love.

So, about those bookends.

PRIORITY

I claim to put God first in my day because I rise early and spend time with Him, but what about all the other "firsts" in my day?

- Am I putting God first in my finances, bringing to Him the first ten percent?
- Is my day planned carefully so that I am living my life on purpose, budgeting my time wisely so I can accomplish things I need to do, want to do and as a disciple of God, desire to do? Or am I allowing TV, idleness, or flowing with my feelings steal what could be productive portions of my day?
- Am I loving others as God clearly commands me to do, or are the activities of my day purposed to benefit me alone?

Do you have a cheating heart? What is your heart chasing? If the affections of your heart consist of anything other than

Jesus, contentment will be chasing its tail. Content for a while perhaps, but true contentment will only dwell if we stop and delight in Him.

Often, I've said that the greatest gift I can give to my husband and children is to not depend on them to give me the kind of love that I desire above anything else. They will never measure up, and that's okay. And Lord knows I don't measure up in loving them the way He can, no matter how hard I try.

Release your loved ones from satisfying a need in you that only He can fill. Release your loved ones to the only One who can fill their greatest desires.

The love of Jesus allows me to love and respect my husband, my children, and others in a way that I never could without Him. I am quick to respond to an "I love you" expressed to me with a rapid response, "I love you more". But the truth is, *He* loves them more. His love always wins.

John's love cuddles my heart like nothing else on earth, but Jesus throbs my heart daily with a vibrating rhythm like no other. Jesus is my Heartthrob.

God's love is not temporary. It is everlasting. His covenant. His promise.

> "I have loved you with an everlasting love;
> I have drawn you with unfailing kindness."
> Jeremiah 31:3 (NIV)

Will you stop for a moment and allow your heart to melt in His love and mercy? Everlasting love. Kindness that never fails. Be reassured. His love is constant. The Lord, our God, loves us so much. If these words don't make your heart throb people, it's time for a checkup.

My desire for you is the same as for myself: that we find true contentment, yet never feel complacent. If we are chasing God, delighting in Him and recognizing His glory, we will always be desiring more of Him. The more we know God, the quicker our cheating heart will recognize when we try to put others (or things) in His place.

COVET

God wants us to have desires and plans. He wants us to be prosperous. He wants us to have strong desires. Here's the but: He does not want us to be green with envy from a covetous desire for what others have. I chuckle when I read Deuteronomy 5:21:

"And you shall not covet your neighbor's wife. And you shall not desire your neighbor's house, his field, or his male ser-vant, or his female servant, his ox, or his donkey, or anything that is your neighbor's." (NIV)

He starts the list and makes the ending crystal clear. Nothing. Nada. Not the house, not the boat, not the swimming pool, not the beautiful lawn. Nothing!

Why? Let's use social media as an example.

Social media has its perks, but one paramount pitfall is the comparison we conjure up when we look at our "friends'" lives. Their vacations look fabulous and they are frequent. My gourmet chef friends who post their perfect, healthy meals for their kids while I continue with my go-to meals from the last ten years. Date night posts in elegant restaurants with wine and mouth-watering dishes, while our date "minutes" are usually riding in the van together from one activity to another.

Do you shut down social media with a sigh, wishing your life was like theirs? Do you think their mountain is higher than yours? Do your "friends'" lives steal your joy?

We not only compare mountains, but we compare valleys too, don't we?

It's not just the perception that everybody's life is better than yours financially, spiritually, or otherwise, but we can also slip into the syndrome of "my valley is deeper than yours." My sweet, sweet friend, if your first response to someone else's hardship is to compare it to a hardship of your own that you perceive as more challenging, draining, or frustrating, you are blocking a blessing. We can't determine the degree of pain in anyone else's valley. Don't compare.

Social media can zap the happy rug from underneath you in a heartbeat. Before you log on to Facebook, Instagram, or any other social media site, remind yourself of what brings you true contentment.

"Measure your wealth not by the things you have, but by the things for which you would not take money." (Anonymous)

Consider your blessings before comparing them to others. Count your blessings on the mountaintop and count your blessings in the valley. The lessons I've learned in the valley are some of my most treasured nuggets and I wouldn't trade that wisdom for anything.

One of our sons had difficulty sleeping through the night. Every night. For years. This child would get up and ramble during the night, so John and I would tag team on Rambler duty or one of us would sleep with one eye open, because our little rambler was curious and let's just say.... experimental.

From the time he came home at 2 years old until he reached double digits, he would often climb into bed between me and John in the middle of the night. For years, John and I were deprived of a good night's rest because when your child does not rest, you do not rest. There were some mornings I would play the guessing game of "where am I" before peeling my eyes open. A toddler bed, the sofa, my own bed or occasionally on the floor beside the resting (at last) rambler's bed.

Those were difficult years for a mom and dad trying to survive on minimal sleep, but for my child, I cannot even imagine the anxiety of not being able to fall asleep, and then, when his body would finally succumb to fatigue, having his sleep invaded by nightmares.

There was an endearing act from said child when he crawled into bed with us. He would take his finger and twirl my hair to help him get back to sleep. He would wind my hair up so tight around his finger and clutch it so that I couldn't budge without waking him up.

One night, he was lying face to face with me, his legs drawn up in the fetal position causing his knees to stick into my abdomen, his stinky breath blowing gently on my face and the grit from his little feet now on my clean, crisp sheets. The locks of my hair wound around his finger kept me locked in for the remainder of the night. I dared not budge else I might wake him.

My husband provided one-man orchestrated music as I attempted to drift back off into some much-needed sleep myself, but watching my child as he slept peacefully, tears rolled on to my pillow as I thanked God for the true contentment in my heart. There was no other place on earth I would have rather been and no person I would rather be than me.

Mom to this stinky-breathed, gritty-footed little boy, who literally had me wrapped around his finger.

As I dragged myself out of bed and dressed myself for work
trying to find focus among the normal distractions of getting
three boys up and at 'em for school, I clutched my nugget.

As I sat around a conference table of fresh faces, fashion
divas, and focused minds, I remembered my stinky-breathed
nugget and would not switch chairs with anyone around that
table for all the money in the world.

Don't be obsessed with getting more material things. Be
relaxed with what you have. Since God assured us, "I'll never let
you down, never walk off and leave you," we can boldly quote,

> "God is there, ready to help;
> I'm fearless no matter what.
> Who or what can get to me?"
> Hebrews 13:5-6 (The Message)

So, Lord. About those desires...

DISGUISED DESIRES

The exposure of our desires can be enlightening. Our
desires will reveal our character. What is the motivation behind
this desire? What actions are you taking to attain this dream?
Some desires and dreams we long for so hard that we would
do anything to get them, but I can assure you that if any desire
you have is not a God-designed desire, a desire that lines up
with His will, you will be disappointed and left feeling empty
once you've achieved it. In fact, we are warned that we can
self-destruct.

"But those who [are not financially ethical and] crave to get rich [with a compulsive, greedy longing for wealth] fall into temptation and a trap and into many foolish and harmful desires that plunge people into ruin and destruction [leading to personal misery]."
1 Timothy 6:9 (AMP)

Many of the desires in our heart are disguised as good, but are actually rooted in evil, causing us to detour our plan. I'm going to use money as an example because for many of us, our stinking thinking conceals the real desire of our hearts, which is to be happy, content, and wanting nothing, and no amount of money will fill that desire. I know, I know, we would all like to test and see if being really, really rich would solve all our problems. I've prayed for that winning lottery ticket too, my friend.

Paul continues in verse 10, "For the love of money is the root of all evil."

The desire to be wealthy is not evil. God wants us to prosper in many ways. Do we want to be filthy rich or clean rich? My definition of filthy rich is selfish rich. All about me, rich. Each time I see the scene from Finding Nemo where the seagulls are fighting over Dori and Nemo, "mine, mine, mine, mine, mine, mine," I crack up. Selfish seagulls! I believe that scene is so funny to many because we can relate to such a ridiculous selfish nature, overlooking the flock around us in need. And don't forget what happens to those selfish, not-too-bright seagulls.

When we learn to be thankful for the little or the plenty that God has blessed us with, we can understand the true meaning of wealth and prosperity; and once the significance of thankfulness sinks in, the desire for more does not go away, but the mask comes off and reveals our God-designed desire to want more so we can give more.

Another disguised desire can be one that is transferred into our hearts from a loving parent with good intentions. My mother so desperately wanted one of her children to play a musical instrument. My brother strummed a guitar for a few years while I stroked the keys of a piano, but neither of us developed the desire or discipline that it takes to become a musician. When grandchildren entered the picture, the desire transferred to them, and now the great grandchildren. Lord, before that woman meets you face-to-face, I hope one of her offspring is labeled a musician. We may need to face the music and accept that even though my daddy's name was Von, we are not the Von Trapp family.

My husband is a baseball fan. That was his cherished sport in high school. We had dreams of our boys playing baseball and one of them gave it a swing for a few innings but had no desire to continue. John was okay with that and we became the proudest and rowdiest ever soccer, fishing, bowling, and surfing fans traveling all over the state to cheer on our boys.

As a parent, you want to see your child achieve the desires of his or her heart, and as children, we want to please our parents, but may end up following in footsteps that we were not meant to tread. There may be disappointment initially when we don't carry our parent's dreams to fruition, but I can almost guarantee you that what your parents truly want for you is happiness and contentment.

Unlike our earthly parents, our Heavenly Father already knows our hearts' desires. He placed them there and will help us discover them, develop them, and delight in them by delighting in Him.

Determined Desires

Determination to get what we want, when we want, is doable. Some people are born with a resolve that would bulldoze a battalion. Others must develop this element of excellence. Be aware that it takes determination and stick-to-it-ive-ness to work a plan and make our dreams a reality, but if those desires are not blessed by God, we will never find true contentment. When there is something we want so badly that we can taste it, our motivation increases, but the temptation to manipulate the circumstances may also increase.

My mantra must be, "Lord, I know that you can, and I pray that You will, but even if You don't, I trust You completely."

Don't rush ahead of God. The instructions are there for us. Trust Him. His schedule is always better than ours and planned with perfection, unless of course, you can tell the sun when to rise, or set the time and boundary of the tides? I thought not.

> "Be still before the LORD; wait patiently for Him *and* entrust yourself to Him."
> Psalm 37:7 (AMP)

But even those desires designed by God will take determination to achieve. This crazy world is filled with distractions that cause our lives to dive faster than a peregrine. Life happens. Marriages are broken. The money runs out before all the bills are paid. Your child heads down a reckless path. The CT scan reveals gut-punching news. Your aging parents lose their liveliness. We lose our focus, or worse, our faith.

We feel drained. We feel hopeless. We feel like failures. Joyce Meyers says, "You can believe that you can, or you can believe that you can't, and either way you will be right."[16] The best news is that we don't have to do it alone.

Determined for Good

Okay, so I'm really showing my age, but I woke up one morning with this song on my mind. Not the wake-up song that I anticipated when my dreams ended, and the reality of the day began. The tune was borderline annoying.

The Sonny and Cher show in the 70's was one of my favorites. They wore the most outrageous outfits and Cher's long, sleek, shiny black hair that she often swirled over her shoulder, could be transformed into as many hair-dos as the hairs on her head. The costumes and tresses alone were eccentric entertainment.

This song, *The Beat Goes On*, a hit for them in the late '60s when I was a mere babe mind you, and written by Sonny Bono himself, had not entered my mind in a long, long time. I googled the lyrics to hopefully satisfy my desire to get this song off of my mind for good, because I didn't' want this "la de da de dee" to linger in my mind "la de da" all day.[17]

There was nothing profound about any words I found in the lyrics. Only that on this day that seemed doomed for dreariness as raindrops pounded on our roof and anxious thoughts pounded in my mind, I recognized that I have a pulse. My beat goes on. And if I have a pulse, then I have a purpose. And, so do you.

On this day, all I wanted to do was pull the covers over my head and hide away, but instead I recalibrated the rhythm and recognized this beat as a reason to give thanks. There is so much truth found in, "Be anxious about nothing, but pray about everything, with thanksgiving." (Philippians 4:6)

Sometimes it begins with, thank you Lord that I have a pulse. Show me who I can bless today, and please Lord, bless me."

On that rainy day, I chose to get up and face what I assumed would be a miserable day ahead. What I didn't know was the surprise blessing God had in store for me that day to bless someone else.

There was a missed call on my phone, then a text message with three words: "Call me, please." I could hear the desperate plea with my eyes in those three words. She needed someone. I didn't need to lay my head on her chest to hear her breaking heart. I knew it was taking a beating and I understood her pain. My heart had taken the same sorts of punches nineteen years previously. I called her right away and her first words to me were barely audible, "I'm having a hard day." I listened as she poured out the pain in her heart. She asked, "Why?" My heart ached for her as my own agonizing memories flooded my mind. I didn't have an answer to her why, but I knew Who to invite into our conversation. I knew Who could give her peace and give her answers. I knew Who could fill this aching desire in her heart. I was humbled that He would use me in a small way to water a seed that had been planted in her heart. God will bless that seed and make it grow.

She was a part of the purpose of my beating pulse on that day, and my prayer is that there will be many pitter-patters of little feet filling her home soon.

DIVINELY-DESIGNED DESIRES

[11] "In Him also we have [a]received an inheritance [a destiny-we were claimed by God as His own], having been predestined (chosen, appointed beforehand) according to the

purpose of Him who works everything in agreement with the counsel *and* design of His will, [12] so that we who were the first to hope in Christ [who first put our confidence in Him as our Lord and Savior] would exist to the praise of His glory."
Ephesians 1:11 (AMP)

Sitting in the pedal pump-up chair of my hairdresser for a much-needed bottle of blonde for my chemically-dependent do and shears to shape my mane, she asked the obligatory, "How's it going?" I was vulnerable and was heaving to regurgitate some anxious thoughts resulting from a gut-wrenching issue with my child.

Years had passed since the day this horrific news scorched my ears and charred my heart, but the particles from the aftermath of this wildfire remain. I spilled tears and spit words about this colossal concern to this young woman I meet with every 6-8 weeks for hair therapy, not heart therapy.

She may have regretted asking, but I don't regret sharing with her because I will never forget the words she said to me when I finished the abridged version of a battle that had been building for years. In a concerned, quiet voice of pity and with a clouded look on her face, she murmured, "Not exactly what you had hoped for, huh?" She might as well have snipped my tongue out with those shears because I was speechless and stunned with revelation.

She was right about the circumstances. No one in their right mind would hope for such, but my life, despite the heartache of hardship we endure, is everything and more than I could have ever hoped for or imagined. My joy is in Jesus and not in the circumstances. I want the Power I have over these circumstances to overwhelm the pity I have for myself on my "whine and wine" days. I want others to see power and not pity. My power comes from this:

- Enormous love in our lives that surges higher than any crushing wave that attempts to knock us down.
- Purification through the pain as we sift out all that stuff that we've stuffed in our hearts.
- Experiencing and tasting God's love and mercy poured onto and into us daily.
- Learning to release others and relish in the freedom of forgiveness.
- And. So. Much. More.

"Huh?" she wondered. But I know. My life is EVERYTHING I could hope for.

Chapter 7

FIRST COMES LOVE

> ³⁷"Jesus replied, 'Love the Lord your God with all your heart and with all your soul and with all your mind.'³⁸This is the first and greatest commandment. ³⁹And the second is like it: 'Love your neighbor as yourself.'⁴⁰All the Law and the Prophets hang on these two commandments."
> Matthew 22:37-40 (NIV)

These words came across to me in an article by Steve Porter with Refuge Ministries. What a beautiful reminder of God's love for us.

"Once I know you love Me most-more than great wealth and more than any other. Once I have become to you a sought-after pearl of great value, I will be your fairest of ten thousand. I am altogether lovely, for I am your King of kings and Lord of lords; your All in all. Let Me bring you to the banqueting house where My banner over you is love!"[18]

I am so in love with Jesus, y'all, and my desire is to love him more every day. I want to bring Jesus joy every day. Even though I was raised in church and in a loving home, it has taken me many years to fall madly in love with Him and I want my eyes of doves (Song of Solomon 1:15) to focus always on Him. Praise Him that He has continued to pursue me and never gives up on me. He will not give up on you either.

"Today, I search earnestly for those who are willing to be doves with a singleness of vision. When I find them, it brings Me incredible joy, so that I can't help but declare: Behold, you are fair. You have doves' eyes."
(Song of Solomon 1:15).

Several years ago, as I was writing out my goals for the year, I became frustrated as to why so many of my goals were never met. Year. After. Year. It was depressing to look back through years of journaling on January 1st (ashamed to say how far back the year) up to the current New Year and see the exact same goals listed. They were all good goals, not delusional, but achievable, however, I was not progressing, not even in one. Why was I stuck? I became angry as I read about the same requests for forgiveness for identical offenses that had kept me imprisoned for years. I cried out desperately to God, "What is wrong with me, Lord?"

A startling question popped into my mind out of the blue, no doubt from the Holy Spirit Himself, I imagined Him shaking His head with a gentle, "Do you love me?" I was reminded of Peter in John 21. Yes, Lord you know I love you. Have you seen my checklist? I did everything a good Jesus-loving girl is supposed to do. Well, most of the time. Church? Check. Prayers? Check. Bible study? Check. Help others? Check.

I tried to be a good person and show love to others. But did I love God the way He tells us to love Him? The hesitation in my answer halted me. Was I showing God daily how much I loved Him? Was I loving Him with my all?

So, let's start at the very beginning. God is love. The greatest commandment is to love God and to love others.

This is God's "Greatest Commandment" and my answer was heartbreaking. Yes, I love you God, but with my *all*? No. My heart sinks to admit this, but it was true. As I began to unpack the scripture of the greatest commandment, I discovered a simple treasure that is so obvious, but it had become eclipsed in complexity as I examined my life. How could I possibly love with my all, when I was not making room to receive ALL the love from the One Who *is* Love. "God is love" (1 John 4:8 NIV). "We love because he first loved us" (1 John 4:19 NIV).

Not only was I botching part 1, but part 2 as well. Yes, I loved others. Some of them. But to love them as myself? I didn't like myself on most days, let alone love myself. I was viewing myself and others through limited vision and I was constantly ridiculing myself, deceived by the lies leaping around in my mind:

- Look at those cellulite dimples and love handles. You will never get that aging body in shape again.
- Keep your mouth shut during this meeting. You are not smart enough or articulate enough to share your ideas and thoughts with others. They are smarter than you and they'll never listen to you anyway.
- Why can't you be like other mothers who have it all together?
- Your house will never grace the pages of Coastal Living. Hostile wins over hospitable. Who would feel welcome in your messy abode?

- You made too many foolish financial mistakes. You will never have financial freedom.
- Your dreams are fantasy. They will never become a reality.
- Don't forget what THAT neighbor said about your child. God doesn't expect you to love him.

The father of lies is the twister of truth and he spins us so fast that our thoughts become tangled and we stagger away from The Truth.

It was not until I started praying for God to show me how to love Him with my all, that I recognized that I was denying God. I was denying His love for me. I said it because "the bible tells me so," but did I *really* believe His love for me?

God created me. He knit me together in my mother's womb (Psalm 139:13). He sings over me (Zephaniah 3:17). I am the apple of His eye (Zechariah 2:8). He sent His only Son to the cross to take on my sin so that He could spend eternity with me (John 3:16).

I wrestle with wrapping my mind around this kind of love, but y'all, if we don't get this, we don't get the gospel at all. We need to believe it. Open our hearts to absorb and accept His love for me and for you.

We start with His love, and once we get it, that amazing love splashes onto others and refreshes them.

"And may the Master pour on the love so it fills your lives and splashes over on everyone around you, just as it does from us to you."
1 Thessalonians 3:12 (The Message)

The thoughts in my mind that I bulleted above were lies that placed a cap on my head and defined my ceiling. The vision of myself and who I am, was limited. But God is not limited. His love is boundless, and his ways have no ceiling. We are not containers with a cap on us, but we are channels of God's love to continually pour into others what God has poured into us.

I needed to believe this in my heart. I needed to see myself through the eyes of my Maker. And what He showed me and continues to show me, day by day, is a beautiful picture of His creation. There is no conceit or pride in that statement because it has nothing to do with me and everything to do with Him.

We cannot love with our all until we fill the holes in our soul with His Wholeness.

You too, my friend, are a magnificent masterpiece (Eph. 2:10). If you have not already realized this truth, how I wish I could take you by the hand and lead you to where that glorious revelation takes place, but I can't. I can only point you in the direction of Jesus, who makes it possible for us to approach the Throne of Grace with a boldness like no other. The place where I delight in Him and where He reveals His love to me. It's where we "obtain mercy and find grace" to help us (Heb. 4:16).

It's up to you to believe and discover the indescribable joy of being ushered into His presence and learning Who He is and Who you are in Him. He will reveal Himself to us and there will ALWAYS be something new to be revealed. His love is boundless. Yes, I know I keep repeating myself, but it is worth repeating because I want to remind myself and encourage you to believe that God loves you and He pours it out to you. His Grace is sufficient ALWAYS. His Mercy is new every single day. Praise Him!

Delight in that, will you?

CHOOSE LIFE-CHOOSE LOVE-CHOOSE GOD

"But if serving the LORD seems undesirable to you, then choose for yourselves this day whom you will serve, whether the gods your ancestors served beyond the Euphrates, or the gods of the Amorites, in whose land you are living. But as for me and my household, we will serve the LORD."
Joshua 24:14 (NIV)

The gift of children has brought me more joy than I could have ever imagined, but the challenges of parenthood has also awarded me the gift of recognizing my dependence on God like no other assignment He has ever given me.

God has allowed me the highest privilege ever in raising three boys. There are no words to express my gratitude for the gifts I have received in my three sons: my greatest assignment. No doubt we have all heard it a gazillion times, but it is so true: parenting is the hardest but most rewarding work ever. Oh, how I want each of my boys to love God with all his heart and soul and mind. I want them to discover early on the gifts that God has entrusted to each of them. My prayer is that they will love and not hate. That they will have faith and not doubt God's love for them. This mama wants joy for them and not despair. And guess what? This is exactly what God has for them and I am clinging to God, tenaciously holding on to what truly matters and claiming this for my children.

[19]"I have set before you life and death, blessings and curses. Now choose life, so that you and your children may live [20]and that you may love the LORD your God, listen to his voice, and hold fast to him."

Deuteronomy 30:19-20 (NIV)

[11]"For I know the plans I have for you," declares the LORD, "plans to prosper you and not to harm you, plans to give you hope and a future."
Jeremiah 29:11 (NIV)

If I choose to teach them by example and not just words. If I choose to intercede in prayer for them as they stumble through these awkward years of trying to discover their destiny. If I choose life, then I will cling to the promise of God that my children, too, will choose life.

Confessions from this mama who tries and often fails: on many days, I fail miserably. There are days that my voice thunders through the house like a raging mad woman. My children will tell you that it comes with only seconds of warning when I declare, "I'm getting ready to blow! Take cover!" Face it folks. Children bring out the best and the worst in us.

It's hard to have a gentle voice when I walk by their bathroom and the stench caused by a missed target overwhelms me. My boys can kick a soccer ball fifty-feet and frame the ball in the exact spot they were aiming; throw a basketball and ring an 18-inch round hole; launch a 14-pound bowling ball 60 feet down the lane and strike all the pins or aim just right to pick up a spare frame, yet stand directly over a toilet bowl and miss the water target. How does that happen? No, really, how does that happen?

It's difficult to zip my lips when my house resembles the aftermath of a tornado within a nanosecond after hours I've spent cleaning.

Why is a trashcan within two steps of your reach, yet the trash ends up on the floor or beside the place where your fanny just rested? Or you missed the trashcan hoop and make an executive decision to leave your fail on the floor?

Why did you wait until five minutes before walking out the door to school to say, "Oh yeah, Mom, I have a project due tomorrow. Can you pick up these supplies today and help me tonight?" And you have known about this project for how long?

These silly things, along with those events that merit a good voice raising and elevated eyebrows, can zap my happy in a heartbeat.

Mama guilt is the absolute worst. Memories of words spewed out that I can never reel back in can suffocate me if I allow it.

Those days that I sent my children out of the car or out of the door with a scowl on my face instead of a smile. Those days that I shouted out, "I brought you into this country and I can ship you out, boy." I don't think I ever said this out loud, but I am guilty of the thought thundering through my head when my anger boils.

When the last words hissed to them as they scurried out the door were, "I told you so," instead of, "I love you so."

Days that I should have been praying from James 1:19 to be "quick to listen and slow to anger." Days that should have started on my knees instead of on my high horse.

Mama guilt is heavy and the hardest for me to hurl off my shoulders. I've learned a few lessons through the years and now know to gab it out with God on the spot and ask His forgiveness, then their forgiveness, and forgive myself as soon as possible. Then I can move on and strive for a better outcome next time.

I must choose to remember all His benefits. His forgiveness and His choice to forget my sins. He has removed my sin. I am released. Satan loves to remind us of our sin and brand us as bad mamas, but God has branded us with a "Yes in Jesus," (2 Cor. 1:22). Remember, God chose to forget it-so let's accept the grace He graciously gives to us.

[1] "Praise the Lord, my soul;

all my inmost being, praise his holy name.

[2] Praise the Lord, my soul,

and forget not all his benefits

[3] who forgives all your sins

and heals all your diseases,

[4] who redeems your life from the pit

and crowns you with love and compassion,

[5] who satisfies your desires with good things

so that your youth is renewed like the eagle's.

[6] The Lord works righteousness

and justice for all the oppressed.

[7] He made known his ways to Moses,

his deeds to the people of Israel:

[8] The Lord is compassionate and gracious,

slow to anger, abounding in love.

[9] He will not always accuse,

nor will he harbor his anger forever;

[10] he does not treat us as our sins deserve

or repay us according to our iniquities.

[11] For as high as the heavens are above the earth,

so great is his love for those who fear him;

[12] as far as the east is from the west,

so far has he removed our transgressions from us."

Psalm 103 (NIV)

MULTIPLE CHOICE

We have a choice each morning before our feet hit the floor: who will have authority over our day? God? Or our flesh? It's our choice to make. God will not force His love upon us.

If you are not acknowledging God first in your day and pursuing His plan for your day, ask yourself why. Maybe things are going well in your life. Maybe, you've got it all together and your attitude is, "I've got this."

No matter my skills, my degrees, my knowledge, so called luck or whatever, I need a Savior.

No matter my vision or plan for the next hour, day, or year, the truth is that I don't know what lies ahead, but nothing surprises God. God tells us that "in this world, we will have trouble, but take heart, I have overcome the world." (John 16:33)

I want to know the Savior of the world and I want to meet with Him and acknowledge Him first every day. Because today, all day, every day, I need a Savior.

If you think you've got this on your own, God may just let you try. He won't force Himself on you. He gives us free will. It's your choice. My desire is preventive living by obeying Him. However, my flesh fails me daily and I find myself in the category of corrective living. The best news is that I can return to God always with my dirty little secrets, receive His forgiveness, and cuddle in His compassion. I have never seen His back, only open arms ready to embrace.

God wants all of us, not just a piece of us. He wants authority because He knows what will give you a full and abundant life. He knows what will fill you and satisfy you. He wants us to confess what is on our hearts and empty ourselves so that He can fill us with His love and guide us through our day. If we don't surrender ourselves to Him daily before our feet hit the floor, then by default we give authority to ourselves and our feelings. Is that *really* what we want? Will you stop for a moment and think about that question?

We may have a plan for the day, but we don't know the interruptions positioned ahead. God does. Stuff happens and hits the fan. Plans change. Some deviations are distractions of the world and others are divine interventions. If we consult God and ask Him to bless our plan, we are better prepared to make decisions that will prosper us, and then we are more apt to discern and greet cheerfully those unexpected distractions as God-designed detours.

Even those unspeakable disasters that slay us. If we seek God first in our day, we are better prepared to accept His healing balm and stronger equipped to help others who may travel the same path of anguish.

The world we live in makes us think that things of the world are what we need to satisfy. We think we've got it under control-no need for a consultation today, Lord. We must have the latest and greatest technology, a picture-perfect house, a flashy car, and the richest foods. We watch television shows and movies that create these "perfect" settings and "perfect" love scenes. We wish our lives away wanting things that will never fill us up and fixations that falter in giving us the genuine desires of our heart.

We idolize things that seem perfect in the world instead of worshipping the Perfect One Who is over the world.

In no way am I saying that technology, nice cars, houses and the sort are bad. The message I hope you hear is that none of these things will truly satisfy. It is only when we "seek Him first," that God will not only provide our needs but bless us beyond measure with desires we don't' realize we have tucked away in our hearts.

"If God gives such attention to the appearance of wildflowers-most of which are never even seen-don't you think he'll attend to you, take pride in you, do his best for you? What I'm trying to do here is to get you to relax, to not be so preoccupied with getting, so you can respond to God's giving. People who don't know God and the way he works fuss over these things, but you know both God and how he works. Steep your life in God-reality, God-initiative, God-provisions. Don't worry about missing out. You'll find all your everyday human concerns will be met."
Matthew 6:30-33 (The Message)

Steep yourself in that Truth.

REMEMBER WHO YOU ARE TALKING TO

We can talk to God anywhere and at any time, but I believe that we should also carve out a specific time to talk with Him before our day begins. I know, I know. Some of you just are not morning people. I get it. But if God has allowed you to wake up to another day to live and serve Him, shouldn't we acknowledge Him before anyone or anything else? Shouldn't we give our first of the day to Him? In Isaiah 50:4 we find, "He wakes us up every morning and opens our ears to teach us." If we have a pulse, then we have a purpose and He has a plan. He will show up. Will you?

Now that I've asked you to wake up a little earlier, I'm going to ask you to do one more thing. May I challenge you to posture yourself in a way that makes you truly aware of Who you are talking to? I promise you it will be worth it all. He is our King and we should treat Him as such. I promise you this, that we find the greatest power on our knees. God is real! Jesus is alive! He gave it all for us and we should give our all to Him. But wouldn't you know it, the return He gives to us is unmeasurable.

When I first started spending time with God early in the morning, I would snuggle up in my comfy chair, curled up with my blanket and bible in hand. Coffee hadn't kicked in yet and I became too comfortable and found myself drifting back off to sleep or at best unable to keep my focus on God. It's good to have a comfortable place to worship and study, but may I challenge you to spend some time in a posture of worship during your quiet time? If you are physically able, spend time on your knees or with your hands lifted high in praise. If you find yourself clenching your fists in desperation, try opening your hands with your palms facing up to receive the love that God wants you to receive. These may seem like simple things to do and I don't know who to credit for teaching me these acts of humility, but I have found that it works for me. It makes me more aware of God's majesty. Don't forget to Whom you are speaking.

As A.W. Tozer said in *Delighting in God,* "Twenty minutes on your knees in silence before God will sometimes teach you more than you can learn out of books and teach you more than you can learn even in the church. God will give you your plans and lay them before you."[19]

Let Him have it all. Empty yourself. The good, the bad, and the ugly. This may take time and that's okay, but don't give up. He already knows what's on your heart, but I believe He wants you to speak it to Him. Acknowledge Him. Admit your wrongdoing. Tell him about that person who hurt you that you can't forgive. Tell him those awful thoughts you have swirling around in your head; perhaps its lusting after someone other than your spouse, anger that Suzie Jones has it all while you're still struggling to make ends meet, frustration that your spouse and children don't appreciate all that you do for them, and yes, even anger toward God because someone you love is suffering from some dreadful disease or coping with a circumstance that is unfair.

God understands our anger and He does want us to bring it all to Him because He wants us to be dependent on Him. Pour it all out to Him and He will pour out His Love on us.

It is crucial that once we have poured out our all that we quickly fill ourselves up with all He has to give us. Fill yourself up with fuel that fortifies. His love, compassion, peace, and mercy. Allow Him to shape you with His grace. Expect it. He will not disappoint. Enjoy Him. Love Him with your all. Delight in Him.

"Trust in the Lord and do good; dwell in the land and enjoy
safe pasture."
Psalm 37:3 (NIV)

Chapter 8

UNFEIGNED LOVE

"True devotion, the kind that is pure and faultless before God
the Father, is this: to care for orphans and widows in their
difficulties and to keep the world from contaminating us."
James 1:27 (CEB)

BLAME ME

We were standing in the doorway of the YMCA gym,
which had been transformed into our Sunday morning
mobile sanctuary, watching the children run and laugh. Two
of them caught my eye as they interacted with each other
and their newfound church family friends. These two were
the foster children of a couple in our church and their laughter
swelled my heart. One had beautiful brown skin and the other's was as white as my own. Two dear hearts were considering adopting these children who needed the kind of love this
family could offer them. Their foster father must have read my
mind. He leaned over and with a smile on his face he jokingly

said, "It's your fault, you know. We blame you and John for these two."

Between my heart swelling into my throat and the forced suppression of tears, I couldn't speak. A nod and a smile would have to suffice. Those words meant so much to me. To know that sharing our story moved another family to love on these children, offer them a safe place for healing, teach them the love of Jesus and consider making them part of their beautiful family through adoption-to God be the glory! This beautiful blended couple already had biological children and were now considering growing their family through adoption.

Our story, written by the Author and Perfecter of our faith, of adoption had touched their hearts, and now their family would blossom and blend even more beautifully. To know that these two children will now have a chance for a forever family because God allowed our story to touch their lives, there are no words, only tears of pure and undefiled joy for what God calls "pure and faultless religion." Lord, may our story, beautifully penned by You, be to "blame" for paving the way to forever families to the ends of the earth. I'll point and "blame" You, Lord for the unmeasurable blessings you are multiplying. To God be the glory!

FOLLOW ME

Followers. Follow my blog. Follow me on Facebook. Follow my tweets. Oh, please "Like" me.

We follow others and we want others to follow us. Can we be honest? How quickly do you return to a post to see how many people liked, loved, laughed at, cried at, or "Oh my'd" your post? Honestly, I really do want people to feel something and "react" to words or pictures that I've posted.

Hence, I write. My desire is to touch others in an encouraging way through my words. I'm an introvert, and conversations, especially with someone new, can be a real struggle. It's difficult for me to feel connected and engaged in conversations with people I don't know. And many times, even with those closest to me.

So why is it we're so quick to follow and fidget to fit in with others? We are born with a desire to belong.

The Amplified version of Romans 3:23 reads, [23]"since all have sinned and *continually* fall short of the glory of God." Because of sin, which I was born into, I am rejected."

But, thank God for "buts." Because of the perfect sacrifice Jesus made for me, I am accepted and will never be forsaken or abandoned by God. Jesus was rejected and abandoned by God for me and for you, but it is only when we follow Jesus that we are indeed accepted. His "like" is the only one I need.

In the past, I have been easily swayed in relationships to fit in with the crowd and be accepted. I wish I could say with one-hundred percent certainty that I have arrived with wisdom and no longer succumb to the desire, or the coercing, to merge with the mob, but I have not. However, with confidence I can now say that I am no longer as easily swayed because I know Who I belong to and I trust Him.

The following is based not on condemnation, but my own personal conviction. Did you get that? Conviction. Not condemnation. If you feel condemnation, please know it is not from God because His word says there "is no condemnation for those who are in Christ Jesus" (Rom. 8:1). God is not wagging His finger at us constantly ready to pounce on us for making wrong decisions.

[1]"Therefore, there is now no condemnation for those who
are in Christ Jesus, [2] because through Christ Jesus the law of
the Spirit who gives life has set you free from the law of sin
and death."
Romans 8:1-2 (NIV)

But He does have His eyes on us constantly because He
loves us so much. We are the apple of His eye. And He gently
convicts our hearts when He sees us taking the wrong path,
and I now recognize conviction as a loving reminder from
my Father.

It's much easier now for me to walk away from gossip or
even interject with a gentle defense for the person who is
the subject of the conversation. I've learned to quickly change
a radio or television channel if the message is not one that
is pleasing to God. And if I find myself in a group of women
gawking at a really buff man, I quickly arrest my thoughts,
taking "every thought captive" and making it "obedient to
Christ" and I turn them immediately to how thankful I am for
my man who loves me unconditionally.

[8]"Finally, brothers and sisters, whatever is true, whatever is
noble, whatever is right, whatever is pure, whatever is lovely,
whatever is admirable-if anything is excellent or praisewor-
thy-think about such things. [9]Whatever you have learned or
received or heard from me or seen in me-put it into practice.
And the God of peace will be with you."
Philippians 4:8-9

Now perhaps you are thinking, Pamela this is a bit extreme,
perhaps even a bit prudish. Really? A group of friends joking

about a good-looking man and daydreaming about the what ifs of time spent with him?

Well, I didn't write God's word, people-He did. And His Way is for us, not against us.

Lust is Satan's stronghold, my friends. What seems like innocent banter between friends or innocent flirting with a coworker, friend, or acquaintance can lead to disaster. One compromise leads to another compromise, and before you know it, you're pulling away from what you know is right and you're over your head in flings that fling us into to guilt, shame, and destruction. Is it worth it?

This message is for everyone. Each of us is one compromise away from doing something we never thought we would, so we must constantly be on guard. We are warned in 1 Peter 5:8 to "Be sober [well balanced and self-disciplined], be alert and cautious at all times. That enemy of yours, the devil, prowls around like a roaring lion [fiercely hungry], seeking someone to devour." The enemy will find the tiniest vulnerable area in your life and attack before you know what hit you.

My husband and I may not be in the best physical shape and no longer have the athletic physique that was so pleasing to the eyes when we first met, but we have built love muscles through the years together for better or worse. For richer. For poorer. In sickness and in health. Exercising those vows to love, honor, and cherish. Seeking God for spiritual fitness has built a physique pleasing to the soul and pleasing to God. We are strong in our marriage, but we remind ourselves that the enemy wants to destroy, and we know we must be perpetually on guard to protect our marriage and our family.

Meet Me in The Middle

My warped mindset used to believe that I had to "have myself straightened out" before I could say with assurance that my life could shine God's light into the world. Don't buy the lie that you must be squeaky clean before the Holy Spirit can fill you or before you can approach God. If God needed clean vessels to fill, he would be out of luck.

I've since learned that I'll be straightening out my life every day until the trumpet sounds or God calls me home. If I wait until I'm ready, I will never accomplish anything that matters for eternity. As we chase God in our daily time with Him, we find ourselves becoming more like Him. It's God's will that we be conformed into His image. Our circumstances don't matter. Our finances don't matter. Where we live or what kind of house we live in doesn't matter. What matters is our relationship with Him.

Thank God that He meets us right where we are in the middle of our mess. He takes our mess, uses it as a message to others and weaves our chaotic chronicles into marvels. Can you find joy in that truth? If you don't believe it, read the stories of those listed in Hebrews 11, affectionately referred to as the Hall of Faith. By faith, some people who were really messed up, people like you and me, were credited with righteousness.

The morsels of mess we leave behind help others to identify with our message. And it also helps us to identify with others and to "love others as ourselves," through the eyes of God. Sharing our story with others opens doors to the kingdom of heaven right here on earth. To think that someone as wretched as me, saved by His amazing grace, can point people to Him is beyond my human understanding, but I will delight in that truth and praise Him.

Jennifer Rothschild posted this quote, "Sometimes God redeems your story by surrounding you with people who need to hear your past, so it doesn't become their future." Oh, how I pray that the revealed mistakes of my past will help many to not do the same. Please learn from the detours of my footsteps. Don't follow in them unless they are leading you directly into the arms of Jesus.

My foolishness led me to waste time, money, and other valuable resources. These were resources that God gave to me and I wasted them by making foolish mistakes by choosing my way and not the High Way. I was not following Jesus.

- My salvation was secure the moment I sincerely asked Jesus into my heart, but I did not keep the commitment to follow Him daily.
- Yes, I believed the truths that had been taught to me since an early age, but was I following the Truth? Jesus says in John 14:6, "I am the Way, the Truth, and the Life. No one comes to the Father except through me."
- I professed to be a Christian, but was I a follower? I could talk the talk, but I wasn't committed to walking the walk.
- My to-do list looked great: Church? Check. Prayer? Check. Bible study? Check. But fully submitted? No.

This has nothing to do with His love. God doesn't just tolerate me. He treasures me and tenaciously loves me. He loves me just as much today as He did yesterday, and He won't love me more tomorrow. God is Love. God wants all of me and He wants all of you, because He wants the best for you and me. He wants body, soul, and mind. This takes daily surrender. Yes, I am a Christian, but my mantle is to be a disciple for Him. My friends, I promise you that He is the only One worth risking everything to follow. This is not to earn my way into heaven-Christ took care of that for me. I must surrender to Him, follow Him, and be totally sold out as a messenger to usher others toward Him. There are so many who need Him.

CONNECT THE DOTS

The more I learn about God, the more I realize how much I don't know. And the more I realize how much I don't know, the more I want to learn and grow. I want God to teach me every single day more about who He is and more about who I am. I no longer want to "find myself" outside of who God says I am. Life is too short for that. We are only here for a fleeting phase and no one is promised tomorrow, so I want to live each day to the fullest answering God's call on my life today. And if I wake up tomorrow morning, I get to do it all over again. I was chosen, and it's hard for me to wrap my thinker around that truth. Oh God, may I live this beautiful life on purpose for You.

"You have made my days a mere handbreadth; the span of my years is as nothing before you. Everyone is but a breath, even those who seem secure."
Psalm 39:5 (NIV)

God's call on our lives is an invitation to live daily for Him and He will shine through us. For me, my ministry begins under my own roof and my prayer is that God will use our story to touch the hearts of those with a desire to love others to the ends of the earth.

My prayer is that my breath in life leaves a gentle breeze that continues from generation to generation. To make that mark, I must take daily steps forward, making good ruts that will lead others toward God, for his Name's sake. God does not need me, but oh how I need Him. Desperately, I want to obey Him so that my purpose will be fulfilled. Our purpose is not a destination, but a daily journey to reflect God's love wherever we are at any single moment of our day. I can work to improve the person I am and help guide others to do the same by following Him, but the message that I share needs no improvement. The message I share is already perfect:

"For God so loved the world that he gave his one and only Son, that whoever believes in him shall not perish but have eternal life."
John 3:16

"I am not the light, but a reflector of the One who says, "I Am the Light of The World."
John 8:12

"Here's another way to put it: You're here to be light, bringing out the God-colors in the world. God is not a secret to be kept. We're going public with this, as public as a city on a hill. If I make you light-bearers, you don't think I'm going to hide you under a bucket, do you? I'm putting you on a light stand. Now that I've put you there on a hilltop, on a light stand-shine! Keep open house; be generous with your lives. By opening up to others, you'll prompt people to open up with God, this generous Father in heaven."
Matthew 5:14-16 (The Message)

So yes, let's follow together our Good Shepherd. Ezekiel 34 tells us that He will not lead us astray. He will rescue. He will give us rest. He will bind up the injured and strengthen the weak. He will provide. He will save.

Forget Facebook and connect with Him today by His Book.

In My Own Little Corner

My favorite song from the movie *Cinderella* is "In My Own Little Corner." One of my memories of being disciplined by my daddy was when I was around 6 years old and Daddy sent me to sit in my rocking chair in the corner (time-out before time-out was popular) for fibbing to him. As I rocked in my rocking chair, I started singing my favorite *Cinderella* song. "In my own little corner, in my own little chair, I can be whatever I want to be." Daddy chuckled and for a moment I thought I had won him over with my adorableness. Nope.

The truth is that I often find it easier to leave my dreams of "being whatever I want to be" hanging in thought clouds rather than chase my dreams and expose failure. Paralysis by fear is a desolate disability. I was too afraid of not being good enough, wealthy enough, smart enough, or pretty enough. So I remained in my own little corner and did nothing, reasoning that I had to do it on my own. Fear almost won. Eventually, I learned that God does not call the qualified, but he qualifies the called. We are partners with Him. We step out and do our part, trusting Him to step in and do the supernatural, and with God as our wings we really can fly anywhere. We can "soar on wings like eagles." (Isaiah 40:31)

"Jesus looked at them and said, "With man this is impossible, but with God all things are possible."
Matthew 19:26 (NIV)

Often our circumstances weigh us down and keep us stagnant. This was how I lived during many seasons in my life. Under the weight of our circumstances we are held hostage by the mistakes of our past or held captive in our thoughts that we are victimized by others who have caused us pain. God does not hold us prisoner by or in our circumstances. My life is living proof that there is freedom in truth that soars high in victory above the circumstances and not buried under them:

- Divorce did not win
- Rejection did not win
- Infertility did not win
- Doubt did not win
- Paralyzing fear did not win
- Words that stabbed my heart did not win
- Abuse did not win
- Abandonment did not win
- Sickness did not win
- Financial hardship did not win
- Death of loved ones did not win

We have no need that exceeds God's power. But we must exert some energy here. We must choose to believe Him, even if we can't see what He's doing. Even if the answer is not what we wanted to hear. Even if-whatever-we must exercise our belief. And sometimes continuing to believe Him in the middle of our pain is a tough workout. Remember, it is a walk of faith. Keep believing Him. He has not let go of you. Wrestle it out with Him. You are working out with a Mighty Trainer and He will build muscles in you that you never thought possible.

While I am still learning to be content and not contaminated by my circumstances, and still learning to rise above my circumstances rather than being held captive by them, there is an overwhelming reality that can leave me feeling hopeless and helpless to do anything.

Each day I am brought face to face, either physically or electronically, with people who need Jesus. As I travel around in my comfortable vehicle with air conditioning and heat, I pass by people who appear to be weathered by unfortunate circumstances. As I am shopping in my favorite super center, I hear a mother cursing her child's behavior and shooting daggers at them with her words. Oh, I've been there, you tired, worn mama, and my heart goes out to you.

It is overwhelming to hear a mother's cries of heartbreaking stories that her child is on drugs, or worse, lost their young life from an overdose. Can you hear the overwhelming cries for help from innocent children born of a mother who was addicted to her drug of choice to sustain her through whatever pain she was experiencing, only to transfer that pain to another precious human being?

Orphans cry and rock themselves to sleep at night and long to be held and to hold onto someone. This wrecks me.

The plentiful pestilence in our world is overwhelming. Cancer, AIDS, mental illness, addictions to alcohol, drugs, and other diseases too numerous to name; and then the horrible epidemic of abuse, sex trafficking, prostitution, and drug dealers. The cries for help pierce my ears and my soul, and the easiest way to stifle the sounds is to ignore them and move on with my life, the voice in my head murmuring, "What can I do? I'm just one person and I don't have the answers. I'm not smart enough or wealthy enough." I'm quite comfortable in my own little corner or the world. But if I'm comfortable, then I'm not growing. If I'm not giving, then I'm not living.

D. L. Moody wrote the following words next to Isaiah 6:8 in his Bible: "I am only one, but I am one. I cannot do everything, but I can do something. What I can do, I ought to do, and what I ought to do, by the grace of God I will do."[20]

"And I heard the voice of the Lord saying, "Whom shall I send, and who will go for us?" Then I said, "Here I am! Send me." Isaiah 6:8 (ESV)

I am sick and tired of that voice in my head that tells me that I can't make a difference.

It's time to recognize who I am in Christ and take a step forward. It's past time to stand firm in the present. My legs may be shaking, but the Rock on which I'm standing is firm.

By the grace of God and to the glory of God, I'm speaking up. Send me, Lord. Use ME, Lord.

"We can do small things with great love."
Mother Teresa

Chapter 9

THE HARVEST

———·—⟨𝒮𝒮⟩—·———

Galatians 6:9 "Let us not become weary in doing good, for at the proper time we will reap a harvest if we do not give up." (NIV)

P art of my heritage is tobacco farming. The disclaimer I must make is that back in the day, the danger to one's health was not understood as completely as it is today. It breaks my heart that part of my heritage has caused health issues for many, including many of my own family members.

My granddaddy farmed tobacco, corn, and soybeans, raised hogs and a few chickens. My daddy, although he worked full time at a local research plant and repaired TVs as a side job (hobby), loved the outdoors and farming was in his blood, so he too, farmed part time. As the daughter of a farmer, I learned the hardest physical work at a very young age. I worked in the tobacco fields cropping, topping, looping, hanging, packing, and on rare occasion even driving the tractor. I may have been the granddaughter and daughter of farmers, but I was a "farm hand" as we called the workers of the harvest.

We would start in the fields in the early morning when dew was still on the tobacco leaves. Tobacco leaves have sticky gum on them, and as you handle the leaves, your hands, clothes, and exposed body parts become so gunky with tobacco gum that it's impossible to clean them without scrubbing hard with hot water and good soap. Tobacco is harvested in the summer, so you're working during the hottest months of the year, especially in the south. We stopped for a short break in the morning and afternoon to grab some crackers with Vienna sausages and a Pepsi Cola. We took an hour break for lunch and never has a meal been so delicious. My mama, Grandma, or Aunt Ruby would have a hot vegetable lunch waiting for us. The vegetables were fresh from the garden and nothing I have ever tasted from some of the finest restaurants in the world compares to fresh vegetables straight from the garden. Corn, butter beans, string beans, okra, potatoes, tomatoes, cucumbers, sweet potatoes paired with fried chicken, roast beef and homemade biscuits with butter and sometimes fried or baked cornbread. Lord have Mercy, that was some good food. And sweet tea brewed to perfection. We asked God to bless it, we ate it, and it nourished our bodies to labor hard the rest of the day.

When not working out in the fields I worked in the pack house where we took the cured tobacco off the sticks, separated the good from the bad and the ugly and packed it in burlap sheets where it was taken to the warehouse to be sold. Working in dry tobacco left one just as filthy as working in the fields. After all, you are inside a tin building on a hot summer day with sweat dripping from your brow and filth sticking to every hair on your exposed skin, lodging in any loose crease of skin exposed.

The fans in place to help cool you off, blow hot air and you breathe in dirt and tiny tobacco particles all day. This may be too much information but blowing your nose after a long day in a pack house leaves no room for doubt what you've been breathing in all day. A hot shower is like a cherished waterfall and there's no need for counting sheep because sleep falls quickly after such an exhausting day.

Farming is no doubt the hardest physical labor I've ever done. As a young girl, I could hardly wait to turn sixteen so I could get a job in a local department store with air conditioning and I could dress up and make fashion statements that didn't require Levi jeans or overalls. The truth is, I treasure every minute I spent working in the fields and the pack house. The prize was the time I spent working with my daddy, my grandma and my cousins, getting my hands dirty and knowing I was part of the "family business".

I have no desire to head back out into the tobacco fields I just described, although I'm thankful for the time I spent there, and the lessons learned along the way. My desire is to head back into the fields God calls me to, whether they are in my neighborhood or across the oceans. Send me, Lord. I want to hear these words from you:

"Well done, good and faithful servant! You have been faithful
with a few things; I will put you in charge of many things.
Come and share in your master's happiness!"
Matthew 25:21 (NIV).

Prepare me, Lord, to head back out into the fields and guide those in need as I am led by the One Shepherd who loves us all.

Huge Harvest

"Then Jesus made a circuit of all the towns and villages. He taught in their meeting places, reported kingdom news, and healed their diseased bodies, healed their bruised and hurt lives. When he looked out over the crowds, his heart broke. So confused and aimless they were, like sheep with no shepherd. "What a huge harvest!" he said to his disciples. "How few workers! On your knees and pray for harvest hands!"
Matthew 9:35-38 (The Message)

When Jesus spoke to his disciples and proclaimed, "the harvest is plentiful, and the workers are few", his heart broke. And I believe His heart still breaks today because the harvest is still plentiful, and the workers are still few. There is much work to be done. My thoughts are that I am not alone in my paralysis of feeling overwhelmed and the impression that my tiny dot of ability and talent won't make a difference. Most days I don't believe that I can make a dent of a difference. And this is exactly what the evil one wants me to believe.

How does one stop this torture of unbelief? For me, it hasn't happened overnight. I've lived with this false humility most of my life, so I must keep reminding myself of who I am in Christ and stop giving the devil a foothold (Eph. 4:27). It is essential that I examine myself and recognize that I am a beloved daughter of the King. I am more than a conqueror in Christ Jesus who steps in and fulfills what I cannot do in each role He has assigned to me. God's plan is victory. The truth is that I can do nothing that God calls me to do without Him. Why would I want to even attempt to accomplish anything without Him? I've tried. I've failed. My prayer is that I will forget those failures and even past victories as I focus on pressing forward to win the prize for which You have called me heavenward in Christ Jesus (Phil. 3:13-14).

Past failures can deceive us and douse our hope for a brighter day, but sometimes worse, our past victories can bring complacency and stunt our surge for the prize.

CRAVING FRUIT

Although I do love fresh fruit during its prime season, you won't find me reaching for a luscious apple for a late-night snack. I'll be the first one to lick the spatula clean of any leftover frosting, but you won't find me scraping out the remnants of cottage cheese before chucking the container.

My cravings are usually pseudo-satisfied with chocolate, chips and salsa, or those crunchy little orange things that unfortunately won't substitute for carrots.

Typically, these food hankerings come upon me when I am lacking something that fills me. Have you ever been caught up in the sweet and salty cycle of defeat? When salty leaves a craving for sweet and then sweet leads to craving for salty again? Which ends up winning? Sweet or salty? After dessert, we southerners may be overheard saying, "Please pass the fried chicken, I need to get the sweet out of my mouth from this banana pudding." Neither the fried chicken nor the banana pudding wins because I am left with a bloated belly, a button about to fly off my waistline like a bullet and a needle on the scales that skyrockets, screaming guilt and shame for loss of self-control in a moment of weakness. That one moment scarfing down junk leads to days of insane workouts trying to wrestle off the weight.

Just as junk food robs us of the amazing nutritious food that God created for us, our junky thoughts rob us of the abundant life Jesus came to give to us.

When I nourish myself with good, healthy foods (or nourishing thoughts), my body is energized and the cravings for the junk food (and rubbish thoughts) vanishes.

What fruit am I craving daily? Is it fruit that lasts for eternity or fruit that spoils quickly? Jesus tells his disciples in John 15:16, "I chose you and appointed you that you should go and bear fruit, and that your fruit should remain."

Matthew Henry's Commentary states, "The joy of the hypocrite is but for a moment, but the joy of those who abide in Christ's love is a continual feast. They are to show their love to him by keeping his commandments."[21]

The fruit to which I am referring is not only leading others to follow Christ, but also good works, which if we open our eyes to see and our ears to hear the opportunity to bear fruit is all around us, in every aspect of our lives. Paul wrote in 2 Corinthians 9:8, "God is able to make all grace abound to you, so that in all things at all times, having all that you need, you will abound in every good work."

I believe this happens in the scope of something as simple as a smile to a stranger passing by to a more brazen act like traveling abroad to place bandages on the spiritual and physical needs of the broken.

My pastor, Chris Woolard, reminds us weekly to go out and shine our light in dark places. Our church was serving with Vigilant Hope, an outreach program in our community that connects believers to those in need. I was on the side of the table serving a simple meal to those who might not otherwise have one that night. As I was trying to adjust my attitude of frustration from a difficult day with one of my children to one of thankfulness for all that we had, my smile was forced and not very genuine. Then suddenly as I looked up from the lasagna I had placed on the plate, my eyes met a stranger across the table and I received the gift of a smile from the frail, elderly man I was serving. It was as if he recognized this mama's frustration and pain through the simulated smile I was forcing. He was so kind and appreciative, but it was his smile that absolutely melted my heart.

He had rugged skin and only one tooth that shined as he smiled at me through his sun-chapped lips. But it was the most appreciative and genuine smile, not only from his lips but from his eyes. I'm tearing up just thinking of him. He had so little and gave me so much. I went out to help those in need and in return saw the miraculous hand of God and I was changed. A smile, my friends, is a good work and bears much fruit. "Peace begins with a smile," Mother Teresa once said, and I left that mission field with more peace in my heart than I had arrived with. And now, when I see someone who needs a smile, I think of my single-toothed, bright-eyed friend and I am more determined to shine a light in dark places with a smile.

Many times, we are blinded to the needs of others by our own frustrations and worries. We all go through awful times. I've been there, and I am forever grateful for the people God placed in my life during those times. Absolutely, we should be recipients of that love, but we should also watch for ways to drape our love around others in need. Yes, the harvest is huge, but God takes the smallest works and multiplies it to reach many. As I mentioned previously, I've often felt paralyzed to do anything because the need was so great and I had so little to give. I'm learning to trust God with what I have, and that He will multiply it to touch multitudes.

Stop, look, and listen. Slow down and take notice of the lives around you: those under your own roof and in your extended family and circle of friends. Put yourself aside for a moment and listen for the cries of the hearts of others. Take notice, genuinely listen, act on what God lays on your heart, and then bask in joy that God used you to make a positive difference. Let's go glow in the dark, bear fruit, and bring glory to God.

My inner fruit, the fruit of the Spirit, must be nurtured so that the outward fruit my life produces glorifies God.

The fruit of the Spirit is love, joy, peace, longsuffering, kindness, goodness, faithfulness, gentleness, self-control".
Galatians 5:22 (NIV)

The Holy Spirit lives in me so these characteristics live in me. When I choose less of me and more of Him, these qualities shine brightly. Daily heart checks are needed so that others will witness these characteristics in my life.

Certainly, the opposites of these traits are not what I desire for myself. I don't start my day out with the following goals in mind. Warning, these seem ridiculous when written out in black and white:

- Detest others. Despise them. Show animosity toward them.
- Parade around in despair, showing gloom and doom on my face and in my actions.
- Be a trailblazer of turmoil and stir up some commotion snuffing out any piece of peace along the way.
- Strangle my joy by allowing the noose of unforgiveness to cut off my circulation to the breath of life.

- Flip someone off in traffic, roll my eyes at the slow cashier in the checkout line, and snarl at my husband and children for not living up to my expectations. Swear under my breath when on the phone with my mother because I've tried to hang up a gazillion times and she insists on telling me that same story...again. (Because one day, if she goes before me, I am going to miss those stories-no matter how many times I've heard them. But in the moment when life tugs at me, I forget how that voice will tug at my heart when she is gone. I can't even think about it and I'm so ashamed for the times I do this.)

- Make deposits of bad instead of good deposits throughout my day. Devote my day to wicked, dreadful, appalling things. Assure myself of making the naughty list. Deposits that are not profitable for anyone, including myself.

- Break my commitments and loyalty to others. Lie, cheat, and steal, and cover up my actions with a sweet southern smile.

- Consider myself above others, put myself on a pedestal, and close my mind to any teachable moments throughout the day. Show reluctance, pride, laziness, and stubbornness.

- Break down any walls that protect my body, finances, spiritual growth, time, and relationships. Flaunt myself about the day unrestrained and assertive, driving recklessly on the highway to destruction.

I warned you. Ridiculous, right? But when I really think about them there is more truth in some of these scenarios than I care to share. Of course, I don't set out to do these things, but if I'm not submitting to the Spirit daily, I'm submitting to flesh daily. My flesh can be pretty ugly, y'all. And without emptying myself daily of *me* so that the Holy Spirit can fill me with Himself, my ugly snuffs out my light to the world. I can't be full of the Holy Spirit if I'm full of myself.

When I see truth in this, I realize how desperately I need Jesus. My true desire is to imitate God. Lord, help me to remember the sacrifice that Jesus made for me. Help me to cling to you, Lord, for You are love, and if I fill myself with Your love, I can radiate that love to others daily. May I leave a beautiful fragrant offering along the way and not a putrid stench.

"Be imitators of God, therefore, as dearly loved children and
live a life of love, just as Christ loved us and gave himself up
for us as a fragrant offering and sacrifice to God."
Ephesians 5:1-2 (NIV)

There is a huge harvest. We all need Jesus. We all need the fruit He provides to us, and we can have it if we have extended that invitation to Him so that we can be workers in the harvest and produce luscious basketfuls of fruit for the kingdom.

"If you remain in me and my words remain in you, ask whatever you wish, and it will be done for you. [8] This is to my
Father's glory, that you bear much fruit, showing yourselves
to be my disciples."
John 15:7-8

WHY ARE THE WORKERS FEW?

The answers provided here by me are the answers to my own self-directed question when I asked myself, "Why? What keeps me from being a "worker" who makes a maximum impact for the kingdom of God?"

So, what is it that keeps me from meeting urgent needs of others daily and sharing the chronicles of my life that may stir them on to love and good deeds? I'll admit that I have a reluctance to share my answers because I have so many regrets of wasted time, of resources, and a lack of effort in my life. Pride, shame, and regret are part of my story, but I suspect that you might identify with some of my answers.

Please hear me when I say that God meets us right where we are and uses us in the middle of our heap of hindrances. I can look back on my life and see that God has been at work all along. But what if we can learn to hurdle that heap of hindrances and land smack dab in the middle of an abundant life? I think many of us are already there, but we don't recognize it because we don't pause long enough to perceive our plunder.

If I can stop holding on to those things holding me back, my hands and arms will be free to embrace the abundant life that He came to give me.

"Blessed is the one
who does not walk in step with the wicked
or stand in the way that sinners take
or sit in the company of mockers,
2 but whose delight is in the law of the Lord,
and who meditates on his law day and night.
That person is like a tree planted by streams of water,
which yields its fruit in season

and whose leaf does not wither
whatever they do prospers."
Psalm 1:1-3 (NIV)

Oh, how I want to be "that person" who prospers in whatever I do. I don't want to just survive. I want to thrive.

So back to the question. What holds me back from being a harvest hand?

BELITTLING THE LITTLE

You know those people who seem to have lined up multiple times in the talent line? The ones who just ooze multiple talents beyond measure? When I compare myself to others who seem to have all the best gifts, I question why God gave some people multiple talents and left me struggling half my life to discover mine. I'm ashamed to admit this, but for years I believed I that I possessed less than enough. However, I now believe, and I will choose to believe daily, that God made each of us with more than enough potential and full of purpose to accomplish great things through Him. I will delight in this truth and dwell on this truth until it seeps into the marrow of my bones.

My heart wants to accomplish colossal work for the kingdom, but my steps to get there are mere shuffles. When I compare my work to what others have done and are doing, my steps stall. "What can I do?" I ask myself. I wasn't born with the drive and determination that seems to be innate in some people. I am learning the lesson to not lessen the value of daily surrender to achieve the tiniest of steps toward my goals. If my tiny steps are paced with wise choices, then teeny-tiny does not equal trivial. Consistency in obedience to achieve my heart's desires can lead to enormous impact.

Ir-Rational Lies

> Jonathan Edwards states, "We contribute nothing to our salvation except the sin that made it necessary."[22]

I don't know about you, but my invoice would stretch for miles and miles. Despite my sins (past, present and future), Jesus paid the ultimate price for each of them. In John 19:30, Jesus said, "It is finished," then bowing his head, he gave up his spirit. Testelestai is all Greek to me, and translated means, "it is finished."

> Continuing from Johnathan Edwards: The word *tetelestai* was also written on business documents or receipts in New Testament times to show indicating that a bill had been paid in full. The Greek-English lexicon by Moulton and Milligan says this:
>
> "Receipts are often introduced by the phrase [sic] *tetelestai*, usually written in an abbreviated manner..." (p. 630). The connection between receipts and what Christ accomplished would have been made quite clear to John's Greek-speaking readership; it would be unmistakable That Jesus Christ had died to pay for their sins."[23]

The commercials for the *letgo* app for buying and selling used stuff crack me up. They are ridiculously funny. Snap it, send it, and "Ta da!" a buyer shows up and takes it off your hands. We already have a *letgo* app for our sins and Jesus has already paid the highest price. We may not be able to let it go, but Jesus died on a cross and *He* let it go forever. If we repent, change our direction and our mind, and turn to God, He chooses to remember it no more. So why do we hang on so tightly to those things that hold us back? Sin separates us from God, and if we are going to prosper in this life, we must let go of our sin and cling to Him.

Referring to the idiomatic proverbs of, "You can't have your cake and eat it, too," and "You can't have it both ways," I personally needed to call sin what it is and stop believing the foolish lies of the enemy.

- My simple pleasure (sin) isn't hurting anyone else. If I'm enjoying myself without hurting anyone else, what's the big deal?
- I can't help myself. It's just part of who I am.
- Everyone else does it.
- I'm not Mother Teresa.
- I've tried. I can't quit. I failed.
- At least I don't (fill in the blank).
- This little thing that I can't let go of isn't really a sin, is it?
- Don't worry, it's just a phase.
- There are no consequences to this sin. God will let this one slide.

Sin is sin. God hasn't change the rules for me and He won't change the rules for you. I've discovered that I can't continue to hang onto my sin if I want the abundant life that Jesus came to give to me. God does not want us lingering in sin and He will continue to discipline us. The longer we linger, the firmer God's hand of discipline will be. He will not let go. He loves us too much.

NOTE: There is sin that leaves us in such bondage that we need professional help. Yes, the Holy Spirit will help you, but He may direct you to a support person, a group or a professional. Seek professional help as the Holy Spirit leads you. I look forward to hearing your victory.

Five Steps-R You Ready to Let Go?

1. **Reveal**-Ask God to reveal your sin. Memorize Psalm 139:23-24 below and start praying it every day. God is quick and gentle to answer. Take time to listen and watch for His answers.

    > [23] "Search me, God, and know my heart;
    > test me and know my anxious thoughts.
    > [24] See if there is any offensive way in me,
    > and lead me in the way everlasting"

2. **Repent**-The Greek word for repent is *metanoia*. Meta (to change) noia (mind). (Strong's Concordance 3340 or 3341.) Repentance includes confession, but don't mistake confession for repentance. To repent, we must *turn from* our sin, changing our direction and our minds. There are times when I turn and run toward God, but often I stumble because I'm looking back over my shoulder to make sure my idol, my stronghold, my sin, is still there. My commitment to sin is stronger than my commitment to God and it turns my stomach

when I swallow that bitter truth. After all, I'm a good, Jesus-loving girl, right? I must learn to think about the way I think about myself and my sin. I can continue to stumble and fall by taking my eyes off Jesus, or I can weaken my knees and surrender, conceding that God's strength is what I need to let go. We. Need. Help. God's grip is firm on you and He will not let you go.

"So here's what I want you to do, God helping you: Take your everyday, ordinary life-your sleeping, eating, going-to-work, and walking-around life-and place it before God as an offering. Embracing what God does for you is the best thing you can do for him. Don't become so well-adjusted to your culture that you fit into it without even thinking. Instead, fix your attention on God. You'll be changed from the inside out. Readily recognize what he wants from you, and quickly respond to it. Unlike the culture around you, always dragging you down to its level of immaturity, God brings the best out of you, develops well-formed maturity in you."
Romans 12:1-2 (The Message)

3. **Recite**-Search for scriptures that speak to a specific sin or a stubborn stronghold, write the scripture on note-cards and keep them close for reference. Where is your cell phone right now? I'm betting that it's close. Keep your scriptures closer. The message you read, when prayed from the heart, is your lifeline to freedom. Secure your lifeline. Memorization is a good goal, but try humbly, simply, and sincerely reading His Word aloud. The pages will turn into a Person. The Word becomes personal.

God's word never returns void:

> [10]"As the rain and the snow
> come down from heaven,
> and do not return to it
> without watering the earth
> and making it bud and flourish,
> so that it yields seed for the sower and bread for the eater,
> [11]so is my word that goes out from my mouth:
> It will not return to me empty,
> but will accomplish what I desire
> and achieve the purpose for which I sent it."
> Isaiah 55:10-11 (NIV)

4. **Remember**-Don't forget to remember. God is at work in our lives and if we look and listen each day, we can see Him. There are many times during the day that I see God at work in an answered prayer, big or small, yet I tend to forget by the time my head hits the pillow that night unless I'm intentional about remembering and recording. Distractions happen. The mind forgets. Keep a journal. You will not regret looking back and seeing God at work in your life.

5. **Repeat**-Repeat steps 1 through 4. Let's commit to this lifestyle. We need God daily to cleanse us, shape us, remind us, redirect us, and nourish us with His faithfulness.

My desire is to be bound by His grace and peace, not bound and determined by a commitment to my sinful strongholds. I choose to hold strong to Him. What about you?

Who Do You Think You Are?

Have you ever noticed that the ninth letter of the alphabet sneaks itself snugly in the center of the word pride? When I look at that word, there it is, pointing directly at me, attempting to conceal itself and causing me to miss the warning signs that this emotional stronghold has on me? Flip that "i" upside down and it becomes a warning! Danger! Danger!

For years, I never heeded the warnings that pride was lurking in my life. Exposing pride is a complicated process and I'm still learning, asking God to show me where pride may be disguising itself in my life. God hates pride and because my deepest desire is to please God, I want to spot pride quickly, confess it, and renew my mind with truth.

John Edwards said:

> "Remember that pride is the worst viper that is in the heart, the greatest disturber of the soul's peace and sweet communion with Christ; it was the first sin that ever was, and lies lowest in the foundation of Satan's whole building, and is the most difficultly rooted out, and is the most hidden, secret and deceitful of all lusts, and often creeps in, insensibly, into the midst of religion and sometimes under the disguise of humility."[24]

Each day I walk a tightrope when it comes to pride and false humility. One foot attempts to walk without pride, trusting and depending on God and not myself. The other foot is challenged to walk without false humility, not believing the truth of who I am, His child who "can do all things through Christ who strengthens me."

Either way, I fall when either of these strongholds sneaks into my sneakers. Thankful that God is my safety net, always there to catch me no matter how many times I fall, and He reminds me that "I am more than a conqueror through Christ."

How does pride keep me from doing Kingdom work?

- Seeking approval from others feeds our pride.
- Pride is trusting in my own righteousness instead of recognizing the only reason that I am "credited as righteous," which is through the blood of Jesus Christ. Believing that if I do everything right and work hard my life will be abundant and effective for the kingdom. My mind must be constantly renewed to believe that it is only through the blood of Jesus Christ that I am credited as righteous. It is by faith and believing in Him that I can claim righteousness.
- Trusting in my own wisdom, strength, and finances is another manifestation of pride.
- Unbelief produces pride.

Let's take a closer look at these bullets with some missiles to help us in our unbelief. We're going to need more than a peashooter. Let's detect and destroy!

"The word of God is living and active. Sharper than any double-edged sword, it penetrates even to dividing soul and spirit, joints and marrow; it judges the thoughts and attitudes of the heart."
Hebrews 4:12 (NIV)

When we trust in the promises of God, we exercise our belief in Him that He will do what He promises He will do. John Piper states, "We don't go to God in belief we will be damned, we go to God in hope of future blessings."[25]

The question is asked in John 5:44, "How can you believe, since you accept glory from one another but don't seek the glory that comes from the only God?

When we look to others to build us up instead of seeking God, we reject God and His blessings in our unbelief.

In Isaiah 51:12-13, God is speaking through Isaiah in this passage and asks us:

"Who are you?" and I add onto that, "Who are you, with your puffed-up pride, Pamela?

"Have you forgotten? I created you. I created the universe. I am the One who has comforted you." Let's get over our self-sufficient selves, and remember and recognize Who He is and take comfort in our Comforter.

Pride is good at hiding, so ask God to reveal your pride to you. He will be gentle, don't worry, but be willing to face the ugly truth and begin battle. When we kill pride, the dark clouds of unbelief will disappear and the radiant beauty of belief will be revealed in your humble hue.

BUSY-NESS OR LAZINESS?

This menacing missile needs to be hurled before I attempt to alter the truth with a flat out lie about myself. Truth: I am lazy in the face of work. Laziness will often masquerade as busy-ness and I am an expert at being busy. One glance at our family calendar filled with sports events, social obligations, doctor's appointments, family events, the list goes on to prove my point. When asked by friends and family, "How's it going?" the buzzing response is, "Busy!"

Everyday life events keep me busy as a bee, and please don't misunderstand me, keeping a family on schedule while juggling a full-time job is exhausting and hard work: managing, organizing, parenting, volunteering, and marriage. Full schedule, but some days my heart feels empty? What is missing and what moves over for it when I find it? I don't want to be loaded and bloated. I want to be filled with contentment.

The work that cultivates sluggishness in me is the battle work I know I'm going to face when I say yes to whatever God calls me to do. It's easy to surrender in the moment during worship when my heart is full, my hands are lifted high, and praise is on my lips. Yes, Lord. Send me. Whatever you call me to do to empty the beds of the orphans. Send me. Use me, Lord! Then something happens between that time of surrender when I believe, "I can do all things through Christ who strengthens me" and the unbelief that follows, right on cue. The scene goes a little something like this:

"Lord, what was I thinking? Did I consider the cost of time, effort, dedication, and work? Do you see my calendar, Lord? Where is the money coming from, Lord? Do you see how much our boys eat? And let's talk about that last battle, those bruises are still fresh. Satan is mean, Lord, and he is ready to thwart my efforts placing doubt in my mind. I think I need some time to think this through more carefully. I'm tired and worn just thinking about it, God. Am I ready to fight it out? I'm not sure that I'm your girl. I'll just tune in to a TV show and tune you out, Lord." Ouch! That hurt to type out that truth.

Drama. Drama. Drama. A live performance from this Jesus-loving girl who desperately wants to thrive and bear fruit, not content to just survive.

My weaknesses scream louder and louder the headline: DEFEATED. This assignment seems impossible, but if I can remember and believe that "nothing is impossible with Christ who strengthens me," and remember that my human effort will never be enough, there will be VICTORY. In fact, it has already happened. We must step forward and claim it.

Can you delight in that?

"Are you so foolish? Do you think you can perfect something
God's Spirit started with any human effort?"
Galatians 3:3 (The Voice)

In "Dew" Time

"For there the seed will produce peace *and* prosperity;
the vine will yield its fruit, and the ground will produce its
increase, and the heavens will give their dew. And I will
cause the remnant of this people to inherit *and* possess all
these things."
Zechariah 8:12 (AMP)

Easton's bible dictionary describes dew as a "source of great fertility," a "symbol of multitudes" (Ps. 110:3, 2 Sam. 17:12), an "emblem of brotherly love and harmony" (Ps. 133:3), and of "rich spiritual blessings" (Hosea 14:5).[26]

We are a society that fancies fast and craves convenience, and I'm usually the first in line.

But God's not in a hurry to deliver to us on our timetable, because He knows what is best for us. Amos 3:3 says, "Can two walk together without agreeing to meet?" If we want to know what that "best" is, we best meet with Him "in harmony" and not hurry out the door to face the day alone. Make an appointment with God and *keep* your appointment with God. Whatever you must abandon (social media, extra sleep, TV) to make that happen is nothing compared to the abundance you receive when you meet with Him.

Yes, God has glorious riches and blessings for us, and He will "give us the desires of our hearts." But don't forget what He instructs us to do first, "delight in Him," and we begin by consecrating (devoting) the fist of our day to Him.

What seeds are you sowing in your life? Are you constructing or self-destructing?

[8]"Whoever sows to please their flesh, from the flesh will reap destruction; whoever sows to please the Spirit, from the Spirit will reap eternal life. [9] Let us not become weary in doing good, for at the proper time we will reap a harvest if we do not give up."
Galatians 6:8-9

Did you catch the phrases, do not "become weary", "at the proper time", and "do not give up"?

Too often, I become weary in the waiting and pray for God to accelerate full speed ahead. But God's tempo is always best, and the blessings are bountiful when we wait on Him. Timing is everything, and Who better to know what time it is than our Creator? He knows the specifics of our place, time and purpose.

Not only do I become weary in the wait, but also weary in wondering why some difficult, dishonest, self-gratifying people seem to get all the attention and placed on a pedestal. We can rest assured, God will not forget. Everyone will reap what they sow.

Let's take a quick overview at the story of Esther. Please read for yourself the story of this orphan who became queen and heroine. It is an exciting story with many lessons to learn.

Note that the timing was after the Israelites had been carried away by the Assyrians as slaves and after the Babylonians had exiled the Jews. Persia had taken over and Jews were brought in by Zerubbabel, Nehemiah, and Ezra to rebuild Jerusalem.

King Xerxes reigned during this time. He was one of the most powerful men in the world. The king was throwing a huge party to celebrate his success of three years and ordered his Queen, Vashti, to come to him so he could show her off to the men at his party (who had been drinking for a week at this feast, mind you). Vashti refused to go, so the king dethroned her.

Mordecai was a Jew of the tribe of Benjamin from Jerusalem who was raising his cousin, an orphan, who was beautiful both inside and out. She was also described as intelligent and sociable. Her name was Esther.

Mordecai took an opportunity to serve the king and Esther entered the king's harem. Mordecai instructed Esther to not let the king know of her nationality and she was obedient. Fast-forward four years (after Vashti had lost her throne) the king chose Esther to be his queen. Esther continued to be obedient to Mordecai and did not reveal that she was a Jew.

Mordecai overheard a plan to kill the king. He told Esther and she reported this to the king giving Mordecai credit. Later, Haman, who was the king's top nobleman, was insulted that Mordecai, a Jew, would not bow to him, and presented to the king a plot to kill all Jews and the king agreed.

Mordecai sent word to Esther to go to the king and beg for mercy. Esther's life would be on the line if she approached

the king without being summoned, but Mordecai sent word
to Esther:

[14]"For if you remain silent at this time, relief and deliverance
for the Jews will arise from another place, but you and your
father's family will perish. And who knows but that you have
come to your royal position for such a time as this?"
Esther 4:14 (NIV)

Esther was at the right place at the right time, "for such a
time as this," and after asking the Jews to fast for three days
and nights along with her and her maids, she agreed to go to
the king and Esther says, "If I perish, I perish."

Please read the whole story of Esther to see how all the
pieces of God's beautiful puzzle fit into this story. Don't miss
one morsel. Everyone reaps what they sow, so be careful what
you sow. Esther reaped everlasting life. And Haman, who sowed
to please his pride? He reaped the height of poetic justice.

"A king's rage is like the roar of a lion,
but his favor is like dew on the grass."
Proverbs 19:12 (NIV)

Chapter 10

SURVIVE OR THRIVE

> "A generous person will prosper;
> whoever refreshes others will be refreshed."
> Proverbs 11:25 (NIV)

I t was our first moments alone with our boys. We had just met them. They were not yet officially ours, but they had already captured my heart. I loved them from the moment of their conception in my heart, which began with a prayer in our kitchen 5,420 miles away and approximately 1 year, 10 months, and 17 days previous, but who was counting?

We had ordered room service and the nannies from the children's home had suggested a porridge for them. They sat obediently at the table and gobbled up every morsel of the savory goo in their bowls. They drank every drop of their milk, delivered to them in a hotel-provided shot glass. Don't judge. We didn't know we were going to have them overnight, remember? Sippy cups were not on my packing list.

They were focused on finishing their meal and my focus was delighting in the twinkle in their eyes, listening to the Russian babble of these 1- and 2-year old little beings, and wondering what in the world their little minds were pondering, left behind in a strange place with strange people who were peering back with pondering minds of their own.

It didn't take long for reality to set in as I recognized they must have been starving. My mind filled with questions like, "How long has it been since they had a meal?" and "Was this bowl of porridge the common chow each day?" Later, as we peeled away the multiple layers of clothes, we recognized how malnourished they were. They were thin, their hair was extremely course, and their skin was blotchy. They did, however, have some stored-up energy that burst forth as soon as they ate their meal. They were a bit wobbly as they ran about the hotel room, but their energy levels increased almost as rapidly as they had ravished their food.

It was heartbreaking to realize we had so much and they had been surviving on so little. We are so very thankful for the care they received, and the resources provided to them while in the children's home. The provision was enough for them to survive, but they were far from thriving. Praise God, He brought us together! I can't even allow my mind to mosey over to the compunction category of, "What if we had said no to God?" I will praise Him every day that I have breath on this earth and I will praise Him when I see Him face-to-face.

RUMBLE TO REVIVAL

"Taste and see that the Lord is good; blessed is the one who takes refuge in him."
Psalm 34:8

It is doubtful that those of you reading these pages have experienced physical starvation, yet how many times after our tummy rumbles do we immediately grumble, "I'm starving!" And I'm guessing you don't hesitate to feed your pitiful pouch until you're satisfied.

How often do we thirst for water, yet find no source to quench our need?

Why is it that we're so quick to quench our hunger and thirst physically, yet starve our spirit?

Is your desire to simply survive, or do you aspire to blossom and thrive and live a life that is so full of abundance and blessing that it causes an inexpressible joy?

Most of us, I think, have been taught that breakfast is the most important meal of the day, and I believe this is true not only for our physical body but for our spiritual nourishment, as well. We regain physical strength when we feed our bodies good nourishment and we regain spiritual strength when we feed on the Word of God.

I am convinced that spending the first of my day with God, nourished by His Word, talking with Him and listening for His instruction, is the only way I will thrive in a world that threatens to devour my desires and perish my passion.

"For God so loved the world that he gave his one and only Son, that whoever believes in him shall not perish *but* have eternal life."
John 3:16 (NIV) Emphasis mine.

Let's excuse the excuses, call them what they are, and join God for a feast that will fill you and will last for eternity.

When our boys got home, it thrilled me to watch their eyes light up when they opened our refrigerator or pantry to see all the food we had stored up for them. Sometimes, they would open the door and peek, just to make sure it was still stocked.

As their mother, I never want them to experience hunger again. I never want them to thirst again. My desire for them is to be well-nourished, both physically and spiritually, so they can be refreshed, energized, and mentally alert. I want them to soar high, humbly.

Our Father wants to feed us and nourish us, and God's nourishment will never run out. Go ahead, peek and see. He has so much to offer us, but we must sit down obediently with Him and partake in this spiritual spread. It's a menu to die for. Gobble up every morsel. Drink every drop.

Jesus tells us to abide in Him and I am thankful for Bruce Wilkinson's insights in his book, *Secrets of the Vine, Breaking Through to Abundance*, that helped me to understand the significance of John 15 and how it applies to my life.

"As the Father has loved me, so have I loved you. Now remain in my love."
John 15:9 (NIV)

The enemy wants us to believe that God doesn't like us. Perchance you have perceptions of God that aren't true. Maybe you believe that God loves you because the bible tells you so, but you argue, "Why would God want to spend time with me?" Do you have thoughts that you need to get yourself straightened out before you can approach God? That if you clean yourself up first, *then* you will be worthy to approach the Almighty?

I've got some bad news/good news for you. You can't scrub-a-dub enough or straighten yourself up enough to approach God. We can scrub and polish and try our best to get rid of the stain from our filthy follies, but our efforts are useless. We attempt to hide our sins and fool others in our lives, but God knows. So tackle those thoughts and tickle your thoughts with this truth: there is only one way to cleanse ourselves and Jesus has already provided the crimson shower that washes us as white as snow. He cleansed us with His blood. God loves you. If you are consumed in sin, He loves you. If you have turned your back on Him, He is waiting to embrace you. He loves you. If you have repented and are living your life fully for Him, He loves you.

He loves you.

He *loves* you.

He loves *you*.

For those of us who know the sweet taste of mercy, we know that these mercies are new every day. And mercy never tasted so good!

..."For all have sinned and fall short of the glory of God, and all are justified freely by his grace through the redemption that came by Christ Jesus."

Romans 3:23

Once we have sincerely asked Jesus into our heart, we want to change our ways to please him. Often, along the way we lose the fire that was ignited early on in our relationship with Him.

God knew I needed a man whose spiritual gift is mercy. My husband is one of the most caring and thoughtful men on the face of the earth. He is the most forgiving man I've ever known. He loves me when I'm irritable, which by the way has happened a lot during the past few years. Menopausal mama has been an ocean of emotion to maneuver these past few years. These emotions mixed with the hormones of three teenage boys most likely left my husband wondering, "Who is this crazed woman?" He has kept his vow through the vexing.

And he loves me when I am, well…, adorable and loveable.

We have few date nights or spend much time alone. This is our choice, because we recognize that being active participants in the lives of our children is vital. We grieve the time we missed from birth to the time they came home with us and we want to seize every possible second with them. We recognize that we are going to blink, they'll be out of the house on their own, and we'll be wondering when will they call, when will they visit, when will they-sorry, I digress.

Thank goodness, the love and respect that John and I have for one another is not based on feelings alone. When we first started dating, I would get that butterfly flutter feeling in my tummy when he smiled at me or told me he loved me. These butterflies now flutter less frequently after almost 19 years of marriage, but our love and respect for each other is constant. Don't misunderstand, I still melt when he calls me in the middle of the day just to tell me he was thinking about me and that he loves me, or when we take long walks on the beach holding hands. No words are needed. Sometimes we're silent and other times we talk. We know love.

When I spend time with God, I don't always get that overwhelming wonder of His presence. Sometimes we talk, other days He speaks specifically through His Word, and occasionally I don't hear Him or feel Him at all. But I know He is with me and I know His love.

When I finish reading my bible or whatever bible study I'm engaged in, I place it on the table or back on the bookshelf until the next time. But I don't place *God* on the shelf. I'm learning to "abide in Him" and "remain in His love" throughout the day. Because I'm building a relationship with Him, I recognize

His voice more clearly. No, I have never heard Him audibly, but I sure have felt my heart racing when a thought comes to mind or the hair on my body stands up straight. I feel peaceful and empowered when I know He has provided an answer to a question I've asked. He gives me everything I need to face the challenges of my day. He always shows up, and many times He shows off and I'm so blessed to have a seat front and center.

We will not experience God's abundant blessings in our lives without actively seeking Him. We can have a Spirit-led life that is filled with abundance or a flesh-led life of existence. If we want the abundant life that Jesus came to give us, we must make room in our life for Him. He will not force us. He gives us space to learn and grow. He gives us grace.

The enemy wants us to believe that going to church, reading our bible, and praying provides all that we need, and if we don't feel full from this checklist of good external things, we must not be smart enough or good enough to reach our fullest potential, or worse, that God is angry with us.

Reading the bible, praying, going to church, and having fellowship with other believers are all spiritual disciplines and good things. But if your desire is to be nourished so that you'll flourish, we must break through and savor every morsel that He wants to feed us.

God's Desires for Us

There's not enough room or words to describe all that God wants for us. Let's dive into a few of them after reading through some scripture from Psalm 23, 27, and 139; Jeremiah 24:7; Matthew 11:25-30; and Revelation 21:3-5 to start.

He desires a relationship with us. The Creator of you and me. The Creator of the universe. The "I Am." The Alpha and the Omega. He desires for us to know Him, talk with Him, love Him, and love others. Because He loves us so.

Start reading. See and grasp all that God wants for you and me.

Prosperity
Comfort
Provision
Love Others
Hope
Future
Fruitfulness
Abundance
Overflow
Peace
Eternal Life
Light
Courage
Solid ground
Beauty
Safety
Shelter
Strength
Wisdom
Rest
Nourishment
Joy
Pleasure
Everlasting Life

Because of His love for us, Jesus shed His blood so that they we can have life while the world just sucks the life out of us.

Are there any of these desires that you want to cross off your list? Need an eraser? I thought not!

Dip into these delights, my friend. Start savoring them and blossom.

"In God there is no hunger that needs to be filled, only plenteousness that desires to give. ... God who needs nothing, loves into existence wholly superfluous creatures in order that He may love and perfect them."
–C.S. Lewis [27]

Abandon for Abundance

"The thief comes only to steal and kill and destroy. I came that they may have life and have it abundantly."
John 10:10 (ESV)

When we become a "new creation in Christ" (2 Corinthians 5:17) we begin to abandon the sin and habits in our lives that ruin and consume us. We abandon the old for the abundant new life that consumes us in Jesus Christ.

When we begin to view the value of prosperity as so much more than merely material blessings, there is an awakening in us that brings new life to the center of our being. We no longer view God as a kill-joy to our happiness, but the One who sent His Son to fill-joy into our lives.

John Piper says, "Tell us, Jesus, what does it mean for us that you are a door for us?

John 7–10 (AMP):

"Truly, truly, I say to you, I am the door of the sheep. All who came before me are thieves and robbers [there have been many who claimed to give what only I can give], but the sheep did not listen to them. I am the door. If anyone enters by me, he will be saved and will go in and out and find pasture. The thief comes only to steal and kill and destroy. I came that they may have life and have it abundantly."

Jesus is saying the same thing He will say in John 14:6: "I am the way, and the truth, and the life. No one comes to the Father except through me." I am the door. If you believe in me, and trust me to be the only path to God, I promise you two things: You will be saved; and you will go in and out and find pasture (John 10:9).

Particularly, you are saved from wolves and thieves that come to kill and destroy (John 10:10). Safe from every enemy that would destroy you. 'Enter by me and you will be forever safe."

But none of us wants to be merely safe. We were not created merely to be safe. The human heart wants infinitely more than safety. Oh yes, safety is basic and necessary. We want to be protected from what can destroy us. We want life. *Life*. But we want more than mere life. We want abundant life. Overflowing life. Deep life. Weighty life. Joyful life. We don't just want to survive. We want to thrive at every level of our human being. We were made for this.

And so, Jesus says more: "I am the door. If anyone enters by me, he will be saved [yes, and more, so much more] and will go in and out and find pasture." The point of saying this is that the sheepfold itself represents safety and protection. But sheep don't want to stay there. In fact, they will die if they stay in the safety of the fold. They want green pastures and still waters.

And I think that when Jesus says in verse 10, "I came that they may have life and have it abundantly," he means, "I came that they might be saved and go out and come and find pasture"-protection and plenty, solid safety, and deep soul satisfaction. Abundant life is not about having stuff. It's about having peace, having joy, having God."[28]

This abundant life is not about being financially prosperous. There is certainly nothing wrong with being financially wealthy nor wanting to be financially wealthy, but do you share your wealth or stockpile it? If you don't share it with others, how does it fill you internally? With pride? With trophies? With a false sense of accomplishment? Remember the twins in Proverbs 30:15-16 "Gimme. And Gimme More." They are never satisfied. We can perish in that kind of prosperity.

The peak of prosperity we live for as Christians is Jesus and He provides plenty. In Him, we are filled with beauty, peace, relationship, and satisfaction. The abundant life of prosperity He gives to us is a privilege freely given. No fence jumping! The only Way to this life of abundance is through the Gatekeeper.

For those who imagine that the life of a Christian is boring, I can guarantee you that until you've been catapulted by God into the wildest ride of your life, you are clueless to the edge-of-your-seat thrilling, the white-knuckle gripping, belly aching, laughter-filled exciting adventures He gives us. He doesn't keep us corralled in the fence, but before you go out to explore, check in with your Gatekeeper.

Chapter 11

BELIEVE IT, RECEIVE IT, AND LIVE YOUR DREAM

1-3"It seemed like a dream, too good to be true,
when GOD returned Zion's exiles.
We laughed, we sang,
we couldn't believe our good fortune.
We were the talk of the nations
"GOD was wonderful to them!"
GOD *was* wonderful to us;
we are one happy people.
4-6 And now, GOD, do it again
bring rains to our drought-stricken lives
So those who planted their crops in despair
will shout hurrahs at the harvest,
So those who went off with heavy hearts
will come home laughing, with armloads of blessing."
Psalm 126:1-6 (The Message)

My life story has so many broken chapters. But despite my mess, my Redeemer has lavished His love on me and allowed me to see tangible miracles in my life. My three sons are at the top of the list. Each day, I am grateful that God chose me to be the forever mother of these miracles and I will continue to write our story for as long as I have breath.

Two beautiful women hold a monumental place in our history, and without their selfless acts of love, I am useless to imagine my life minus the miracles they birthed. Although I've never met either one of them, my heart overflows with gratitude that they chose life for our three sons. We have papers with words that describe minimally the details of the circumstances they faced over fifteen years ago, and portions of their story could trigger judgement from me. I choose love. I do not know if they acted in fear or in courage, but this I believe with all my heart-they acted in love.

They left their babies at an altar trusting someone for a better life for them. God saw these women and watched over their wombs filled with wonder. God harmonized her cry with my own and I am speechless to utter significant praise to Him. My prayer is for peace in their hearts to know the joy they birthed into our lives. My hope is to meet them one day so they can see for themselves the tangible miracles of God's Hand. Forever, I am grateful.

When I remember what Jesus did for me and His compassion for me (and for you), I am moved to action. This thing called love that God commands us to do is a verb. An action. "He loved us so much that He *sent.*" (John 3:16) Emphasis mine. He calls us as His disciples to act, but before He calls us into action, He calls us to be with Him. Sitting with Jesus and getting to know Him will equip us with wisdom and power to step out in our faith.

God will guide us. Guiding indicates that you must take some steps of your own. We are partners with God in this life of ours. The lesson I've learned over these past few years is that I must plan for my desires. I must plan for those doors and opportunities that don't swing open as quickly as I would like, and for those doors and opportunities that are slammed shut. The most important plan is to spend my time with the One who will direct and establish my steps. I won't stop knocking or asking if I believe my desires are attuned with God's heart.

Make room for God in your life. Don't just pencil Him in on your calendar. Mark Him in with a permanent marker. Talk to God about your plans. Design your plans. Use your God-given creativity and intelligence to design your unique, beautiful plans. Sketch them out. Expect God to help you, but don't limit your expectations of how He will help you. Then hold on as God propels you. He will take your sketches and turn them into amazing portraits that are more beautiful than you could ever imagine. These portraits will reveal your radiant semblance of His image. People will notice that you really do favor your Father.

Drop the mic and delight in that, people.

Vested Plan Percentage?

We are partners with God, not puppets on a string. He wants us to be full participants in His plan, but He gives us free will to choose.

A quote from C. S. Lewis:

> "God created things which had free will. That means creatures which can go wrong or right. Some people think they can imagine a creature which was free but had no possibility of going wrong, but I can't. If a thing is free to be good, it's also free to be bad. And free will is what

has made evil possible. Why, then, did God give them free will? Because free will, though it makes evil possible, is also the only thing that makes possible any love or goodness or joy worth having. A world of automata-of creatures that worked like machines-would hardly be worth creating. The happiness which God designs for His higher creatures is the happiness of being freely, voluntarily united to Him and to each other in an ecstasy of love and delight compared with which the most rapturous love between a man and a woman on this earth is mere milk and water. And for that they've got to be free. Of course, God knew what would happen if they used their freedom the wrong way: apparently, He thought it worth the risk. (...) If God thinks this state of war in the universe a price worth paying for free will-that is, for making a real world in which creatures can do real good or harm and something of real importance can happen, instead of a toy world which only moves when He pulls the strings-then we may take it is worth paying."[29]

We can choose to sit around and daydream about our desires in a fantasy world or we can be determined to achieve our heart's desires in the real world. The choice is ours. He will give us direction and give us strength which leads us to victory.

"For the eyes of the Lord range throughout the earth to strengthen those whose hearts are fully committed to him."
2 Chronicles 16:9 (NIV)

Are you waving your hands in the air, saying, "Here I am, Lord?" Or are you crouched in a corner trying to hide in the shadows?

Thank God, I've learned, and I am still growing, but the popular plan of my life used to be flying by the seat of my pants. Like Wrongway Corrigan, I decided a course of action along the way instead of following a predetermined plan. There were a few exceptions that exhibited my organizational skills of being a following the rules, crossing my t's and dotting my i's, kind of gal.

God is a God of order and not chaos. He has a plan, and we should have a plan and pray that He blesses it if it is good.

"God doesn't stir us up into confusion; he brings us
into harmony."
1 Corinthians 14:33 (The Message)

CONTINGENCY PLAN

Our plans fail. Our plans falter. Doors close. Life happens. And sometimes your plan or desire may be disguised or designed differently than you imagined. Don't forget that God may interrupt your plan for His purpose, and His purpose is always good.

God's plan is Plan A is for all His people. God's design is always amazing.

Sometimes, something needs to change in us before God will work through us.

Many of the dreams of my past that never came to be I can shout out praises that God slammed those doors shut. Others, I will never know why until I see Him face-to-face. There is one desire in my heart that remains and for years I have felt like a caged lioness, pacing back and forth, panting frantically, "Let me out, Lord. I'm ready." Thank God, He won't open the cage door too soon, because He knows my plan will falter until I'm ready. I'm good with God on that one. If He says I'm not ready, then toss the key.

Perhaps God is preparing the hearts of people for whose paths I'll cross to receive the seed to be planted. Maybe you're waiting on God, too, wondering why your plan has not come to fruition. What will you do during the wait?

What is the contingency strategy for the Nos and the Not yets? Maybe God slammed a door shut. There's a reason, and part of our faith journey is to trust in God and recognize that His reason is a good one.

Bloom where you're planted right now. Today, deposit good in the lives of others. There's your purpose in life, people. Learn and grow, fertilize and nurture your desires. Gain knowledge on what to weed out and what to water. Persevere. Keep on keeping on. Keep on growing. Keep on asking and seeking and knocking.

"Ask and keep on asking and it will be given to you; seek and keep on seeking and you will find; knock and keep on knocking and the door will be opened to you."
Matthew 7:7 (AMP)

God will answer you if you ask and believe, and we must believe that His answer is His best for us. To seek indicates that we must add to our asking our due diligence of pursuing. Keep on knocking and the door will be opened at just the right time, and when you get a peek as the door is opened, be ready to be WOWed!

If your plot has reached a dead end, there may be life beginning right around the corner. Don't give up. Recognize that God's refusal to open a specific door or slam one shut on you is because He loves you too much to allow it for now, or perhaps ever.

Redirection or recalibration could be all you need. If you have reached a crossroad and don't know which direction to take, stop and rest for a while. God will show you whether to turn right, left, go straight, or wait. He wants our focus on Him. Enjoy this time of waiting on Him. Grow. Take time to remember your journey thus far and the lessons you've learned along the way. Ask God to refresh you, continue to shape you, and prepare you for the rest of the wild ride ahead. Being still is hard and God knows that it's hard for us, but sometimes we must stop. Be still. And breathe. Refresh ourselves because we have a race to finish. There is much to be accomplished in this world. You are needed. You have a purpose. Don't allow life to breeze by you. Live it on purpose.

This is the final chapter of this book, but not my final chapter in life. There are many dreams and desires yet to be discovered and developed, but with determination and divine power, anything is possible.

"I can do all things [which He has called me to do] through Him who strengthens and empowers me [to fulfill His purpose-I am self-sufficient in Christ's sufficiency; I am ready for anything and equal to anything through Him who infuses me with inner strength and confident peace]"
Philippians 4:13 (AMP)

There was a seed planted in my early years that has been watered and fertilized by many and continues to grow. I frequented a small country church with a beautiful, simple steeple with my Aunt Ruby and Uncle Wesley. Memories of singing beautiful hymns in my home church as well as that sweet, small country church remain in my heart. Surrounded by beautiful stained-glass windows and wooden pews, holding hymnals that contained masterpieces of music, we belted out old hymns. I remember staring straight ahead at the altar as we sang songs like, "Oh, How I Love Jesus," where the stained-glass window of Jesus holding a little lamb mesmerized me and I would imagine Jesus holding me.

There is one song that lingers in my mind today, and if I listen carefully, I can hear my Grandma, Aunt Ruby, and my sweet Mama singing it now.

I love to tell the story
Of unseen things above
Of Jesus and his glory
Of Jesus and his love
I love to tell the story
Because I know 'tis true
It satisfies my longings
As nothing else can do
I love to tell the story
'Twill be my theme in glory
To tell the old, old story
Of Jesus and his love
I love to tell the story
For those who know it best
Seem hungering and thirsting
To hear it like the rest
And when in scenes of glory
I sing the new, new song
'Twill be the old, old story
That I have loved so long
I love to tell the story

'Twill be my theme in glory
To tell the old, old story
Of Jesus and his love
To tell the old, old story
Of Jesus and his love
Songwriters: Katherine Hankey, William G. Fischer
© Public Domain
For non-commercial use only.
Data From: LyricFind

My childhood desire to belt out twangy tunes may have faded away, but as I grow to fill my mantle as a disciple of Christ, I have a number-one burning desire to belt out God's love to the world.

The adoption seed that was planted early in my life long before I could comprehend the splendor that the seed would produce has come to fruition. Now that I know the wonder of God's adoption of me and the joy that has saturated our lives by adopting our boys, my second-greatest kingdom desire is that orphan beds are emptied all over the world and each of those beautiful children will carry that label no longer. I pray that they will be marked instead by kisses, hugs and love from loving families and snuggled safely into beds of their very own, kissed goodnight by loving mothers and fathers and truly experience sweet dreams. I pray that fears are doused and those called will step out and enjoy the blessings of the amazing orchestration of adoption. Until they are all home, I will pray.

"God sets the lonely in families..."
Psalm 68:6

If a seed of adoption has been planted in your heart, don't allow the weeds of fear to strangle its growth. Don't listen to the liar. Ask questions. Explore the possibility. What if *your* child is waiting? Don't miss the moment and miss your blessing.

You will almost always feel fear when you say yes to God, knowing that it's something so big that only He can do it. Your trust must be completely in Him, and the thrill of tagging along on the ride with His powerful Hand guiding you along the way is exhilarating. Imagine the smile on God's face when you say, "Yes."

As Christians, we have this amazing opportunity to channel God's love in so many ways. What will you do to open your life and family to help others? Will you open your heart to God's desires and His plan? Each of us has an chance to be a part of someone's story. Our family gets a front row seat every day as we literally get to see how God set three lonely little boys into our lives. He settled this mama's heart as a happy mother of children (Psalm 113:9). God's word is true. His promises are real. It's a beautiful sight to see.

TIMELESS PLAN

My story is not over, and if you are reading this, neither is yours.

Even if God zaps me outta here in the next tap of the keyboard, my beat goes on. I may flatline in my earthly body, but by the resurrection power of Jesus, there is a happily forever after waiting for me and Chapter One will begin.

C.S. Lewis says, "Chapter One of the Great Story which no one on earth has read: which goes on forever: in which every chapter is better than the one before."[30]

My prayer is that the miniscule dot of a positive difference I make while I am here will connect with other dots that pave the way straight to Jesus. Will you join me?

My friends, my prayer for you is that the ray of vision for your life travels radically past the white picket fence, wrought iron gate, or any other barricade that keeps you from the dreams and desires that God has for you. Maybe your fence is invisible to your eyes, but your fears detect it and when you try to move past that barrier, fear zaps you and you remain paralyzed, secluded, and pseudo-satisfied in your own little corner of the world. Satan wants to keep you there, my friend.

There is hope.

Jesus came to die for us so that we can have life for eternity, but He also came to teach us how to live in this crazy, far from perfect world. Thank God this is not our forever home. Our perfect home awaits.

"Jesus told this simple story, but they had no idea what he was talking about. So, he tried again. "I'll be explicit, then. I am the Gate for the sheep. All those others are up to no good-sheep stealers, every one of them. But the sheep didn't listen to them. I am the Gate. Anyone who goes through me will be cared for-will freely go in and out and find pasture. A thief is only there to steal and kill and destroy. I came so they can have real and eternal life, more and better life than they ever dreamed of."
John 10:6-10 (MSG)

He came so that we may have abundant life, a life we could never dream of ourselves. Don't let fear rob you. Sidestep pity, plug into His power, and persevere. Enjoy Him so that you can enjoy your life.

Let's raise the roof, people, and lead the parade with our banners. (Psalm 20:5 The Message) I am on the edge of my seat waiting to hear your story.

> [4] "May he give you the desire of your heart
> and make all your plans succeed.
> [5] May we shout for joy over your victory
> and lift up our banners in the name of our God."
> Psalm 20:4-5 (NIV)

ENDNOTES

1 A.W. Tozer, Delighting in God, (Bethany House, a division of Baker Publishing Group, Minneapolis, Minnesota), 17

2 Mark Batterson, If - Trading Your If Only Regrets for God's What If Possibilities, (Baker Books, Grand Rapids, Michigan), 15.

3 Charles Stanley, Holding on To Our Hope, (In Touch Daily Devotional),

https://www.lightsource.com/devotionals/in-touch-with-charles-stanley/in-touch-05-08-04-1260903.html

4 Bruce Wilkinson, The Prayer of Jabez, (Multnomah Publishers, Inc, Sisters, Oregon), 26-27.

5 https://www.faithgateway.com/the-best-yes-youve-got-a-part-to-play/#.XABGh_ZFxfw

6 https://www.beliefnet.com/faiths/christianity/christmas/the-gift-of-a-child.aspx

7 https://www.bing.com/search?q=current+number+of+orphans+in+the+world&form=EDNTHT&mkt=en-us&httpsmsn=1&refig=75c09dd3968b4640b05dea10431df0ab&PC=DCTE&sp=-1&pq=current+number+of+orphans+in+the+world&sc=0-38&qs=n&sk=&cvid=75c09dd3968b4640b05dea10431df0ab

8 Beth Moore, Believing God, (LifeWay Press, Nashville, TN), 139.

9 Beth Moore, Believing God, (LifeWay Press, Nashville, TN), 139.

10 A.W. Tozer, Delighting in God, (Bethany House, a division of Baker Publishing Group, Minneapolis, Minnesota), 15.

11 Rick Warren, The Purpose Driven Life, What On Earth Am I Here For?, (Zonderan, Grand Rapids, Michigan), 63.

12 Rick Warren, The Purpose Driven Life, What On Earth Am I Here For?, (Zonderan, Grand Rapids, Michigan),78.

13 A.W. Tozer, Delighting in God, (Bethany House, a division of Baker Publishing Group, Minneapolis, Minnesota)

14 https://www.youtube.com/watch?v=vDs57R6MYsY

15 Bruce Wilkinson, Secrets of the Vine, (Multnomah Publishers, Inc, Sisters, Oregon), 53

16 Joyce Meyer, Seize the Day, (FaithWords, Hatchette Book Group, New York, NY), 78

17 https://www.bing.com/search?q=lyrics+to+the+beat+goes+on&-form=EDGTCT&qs=PF&cvid=1a2da0bb-f6e04922b7ee0c586ae87868&refig=4d4393406f9345578 37e5f4b1c10e3a5&cc=US&setlang=en-US&PC=DCTE

18 http://www.elijahlist.com/words/display_word.html?ID=20897

19 A.W. Tozer, Delighting in God, (Bethany House, a division of Baker Publishing Group, Minneapolis, Minnesota), 87.

20 http://ministry127.com/resources/illustration/god-can-use-one

21 https://www.biblestudytools.com/commentaries/matthew-henry-complete/john/15.html

22 https://www.azquotes.com/author/4377-Jonathan_Edwards

23 https://bible.org/question/what-does-greek-word-tetelestai-mean

24 https://www.azquotes.com/author/4377-Jonathan_Edwards

25 https://www.desiringgod.org/

26 https://www.biblestudytools.com/dictionaries/eastons-bible-dictionary/dew.html

27 C. S. Lewis, The Four Loves (New York: Hardcourt Brace Jovanovich, 1960), 175.

28 https://www.desiringgod.org/messages/my-abandoned-life-for-your-abundant-life--2

29 https://www.goodreads.com/quotes/437424-god-created-things-which-had-free-will-that-means-creatures

30 https://www.goodreads.com/quotes/1213936-now-at-last-they-were-beginning-chapter-one-of-the

CPSIA information can be obtained
at www.ICGtesting.com
Printed in the USA
BVHW031732110320
574751BV00001B/43